Learn to Program Using Python

A Tutorial for Hobbyists, Self-Starters, and All Who Want to Learn the Art of Computer Programming

Alan Gauld

ADDISON–WESLEY

Boston • San Francisco • New York • Toronto • Montreal
London • Munich • Paris • Madrid
Capetown • Sydney • Tokyo • Singapore • Mexico City

The publisher offers discounts on this book when ordered in quantity for special sales. For more information, please contact:

Pearson Education Corporate Sales Division
One Lake Street
Upper Saddle River, NJ 07458
(800) 382-3419
corpsales@pearsontechgroup.com

Visit us on the Web at www.awl.com/cseng/

Library of Congress Cataloging-in-Publication Data

Gauld, Alan.
    Learn to program using Python: a tutorial for hobbyists, self-starters, and all who want to learn the art of computer programming / Alan Gauld.
        p. cm.
    Includes bibliographical references and index.
    ISBN 0-201-70938-4 (alk. paper)
    1. Python (Computer program language) I. Title.

QA76.73.P48 G38 2000
005.13'3--dc21   00-046921

ISBN 0-201-70938-4

Text printed on recycled and acid-free paper.
ISBN 0201709384

In memory of my grandmother,
who loved reading and
died during the writing of this book.

Contents

Section 3   Advanced Topics

Section 4   Case Studies

Appendices

Preface

Why Write This Book?

I started this tutorial in response to a request from two friends, both of whom were proficient computer users but wanted to go a step further and learn to program. As both had Internet access, I decided to save myself some trouble and find an online tutorial that they could use. Much to my amazement, this quest came up empty—it proved very difficult to find a tutorial that addressed the needs of an absolute beginner. Many tutorials taught specific programming languages, but they all assumed prior programming knowledge. This exercise provided sufficient motivation for me to create my own online tutorial for beginners. (You can see the online version at `http://www.crosswinds.net/~agauld/`. It's also on the CD-ROM as a Zip file.) I had assumed that 10 to 20 pages would suffice, but the project grew and grew. Soon I had more than 50 pages of printout and was getting increasing numbers of visitors to my Web site, many of whom asked questions or required clarification of points. Responding to their requests, in turn, improved the quality and expanded the volume still further. Several readers suggested that the tutorial would make a useful book, and this text is the result.

My Background

I am a professional programmer who came to programming from an electronic engineering background. I've been involved with computers and the information technology industry since the mid-1970s, working on everything from embedded microcontrollers to mainframe billing systems. In that time I have used (and continue to use) several computer languages and operating systems.

A Word about Languages

For commercial reasons I have tried to use American English spellings and terminology throughout the book. This choice has led to some interesting discoveries about the differences between how American English and the rest of the English-speaking world do things. For those non-Americans who get irritated at the inexorable pollution of the Queen's English, I proffer my apologies and sympathy, but I hope you buy the book anyway! To U.S. readers, I hope that any remaining Anglicisms are not too offensive or confusing. Please consider them a quaint relic from the past.

Acknowledgments

As ever, this book's existence owes a lot to many people. In particular, I'd like to thank Ray and John, who started the ball rolling, as well as all the folks who visited and commented on the original online tutorial. Also meriting a mention are Matthew Curtin and Herb Sutter, both of whom urged me to "go for it," and Jeff, my boss at work, whose support further encouraged me. Next must come Mike Hendrickson and Heather Peterson, my editors at Addison-Wesley, who were never less than enthusiastic about the project. Finally, I'd like to thank Matt, Dave, Brian, Moira, and Perdita, who have been press-ganged into reviewing various drafts or had ideas bounced off them. I'd also like to thank the many technical reviewers whose comments have helped shape the direction of the book. They all spotted many mistakes; any that remain behind are solely mine. Finally, thanks to my wife, Heather, who patiently whiled away the many hours alone as I gazed haplessly at the PC.

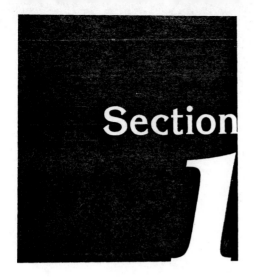

Section

1

Introduction

In this section we look at the focus of this book, the basic concepts and history of programming, and the prerequisites both for reading the book and for becoming a successful programmer. We also briefly consider the programming language and environment we will be using.

Chapter

1

Who, What, and How?

What will we cover?

- *The intended audience*
- *What will be discussed*
- *How the book should be read*
- *How the book is organized*

Who Is Programming For?

In recent years many people, like the two friends mentioned in the preface, have bought personal computers and become involved in computing. At the same time, businesses have become IT-enabled and have often appointed nonspecialist but enthusiastic users as systems administrators and mentors to their colleagues. In parallel with these trends, the Internet has exploded in popularity, bringing another wave of new computer users. Members of each of these three groups have, eventually, come upon situations where the standard software packages cannot meet the requirements being placed on them. These limitations either are just accepted as inherent limits on what can be achieved or provide the motivation for users to break through the perceived barriers to computing and become a programmer.

These problem situations can manifest themselves in several forms:

- A program is needed but nothing suitable seems to be available in software stores or on the Internet.

- An existing application needs to be customized in a way that can't be done using simple record/playback-type macros.

- The user desires to create a Web site with fancy dynamic content, like the ones seen while he or she is surfing the Web. Unfortunately, basic HTML, as produced by most WYSIWYG editors, doesn't provide the power or flexibility to support this type of development.

Any or all of these situations may provide the motivation to "take control," which ultimately means learning to program. On the other hand, curiosity to find out what "hacking" is all about[1] may be the driving force behind a person's decision to become a programmer.

The reader of this book is therefore likely to be an experienced computer user, probably with several years of experience in using a computer with MS-DOS and/or Microsoft Windows, and possibly Linux or another UNIX variant. You might even be a systems administrator with Microsoft or Novell certification (MSCE or CNE) but no programming experience. I also expect you to understand some rudimentary mathematical concepts such as elementary logic and basic algebra. I won't apologize for this assumption because programming is rooted in a mathematical tradition and many of its underlying concepts have corresponding mathematical ideas. Having said that, the depth of knowledge required is not very great. You can probably just skim over the bits you don't understand and still follow most of what's happening.

What Will This Book Cover?

This book covers the basic theory of computer programming—its definition, some of its history, and the fundamental techniques needed to solve problems. It will not describe esoteric techniques or the details of any particular programming language. Although the bulk of the material will use a language called *Python*.[2] One of my chief aims in this book is to emphasize that

---

1. Hacking *historically means a kind of intensive programming activity and has nothing to do with breaking into other computer systems. Real hackers prefer to use the term "cracking" to describe the latter activity. I use the term "hacking" strictly in its programming sense.*
2. *Python is not named after the snake family but rather after the BBC TV series:* Monty Python's Flying Circus. *If you're a fan, you'll recognize occasional references to sketches from the series. This homage has become something of a tradition amongst Python programmers.*

programming is not about any particular language. Instead, programming seeks to represent a problem using a few key constructs and then translate those constructs into whichever language is most suitable for the problem.

This book will not cover issues like ways to create or copy text files, installation of every software package mentioned, or the organization of the computer's file system. Frankly, if you need to know those things, then you probably are not ready to program. Try to find a tutorial for your computer and operating system and keep it handy as you work through the book. If you come across a concept you don't understand in this book, you can then check your computer tutorial to find out how to do it.

Why Python?

Python is a nice language to learn. Its syntax is simple, and some very powerful features are built into the language. Phython supports lots of programming styles, from the very simple to state-of-the-art object-oriented programming techniques. The language runs on lots of platforms: UNIX/ Linux, Microsoft Windows, Macintosh, and several more. In additon, it has a very friendly and helpful user community available via several mailing lists[3] and an active Internet news group.[4] Finally it's free and therefore accessible to anyone regardless of economic circumstance. All of these characteristics are very valuable qualities in a beginner's language.

Python, however, is not *just* a beginner's language. As your experience grows, you can continue using Python as either an end in itself or a rapid prototyping tool. Python is not suitable for a few things, but they are comparatively rare and specialized. The real message of this book is that while Python is nice, it's not the only way to write programs.

How to Read This Book

This book includes several features intended to help the reader extract what's needed. The main text concentrates on teaching fundamental concepts using Python as a demonstration language. In addition, numerous sidebars contain conceptual or background information that is not essential to understanding the main flow of the text. If you are in a hurry, you can

---

3. *The mailing lists can be found on the Python Web site* `http://www.python/org`.
4. *The news group is* `comp.lang.python`.

simply ignore the sidebars and reduce the amount of reading to be done. You probably should come back and read the sidebars later, because they do contain some useful information.

You should realize that this book is not a complete tutorial for Python. Alternative ways of doing things might exist that are faster or easier than the techniques demonstrated here. Remember, I'm trying to teach you how to program—not how to best use any particular language. Python includes a full tutorial as part of its standard documentation, and I strongly advise you to work through it after completing this book. The book will provide the necessary background to understand the tutorial. Just as important, however, is that you should be ready to work through the tutorial for any other language after completing this text. The concepts you learn in this book will make learning another language a quick and painless exercise.

Each chapter begins with a brief statement of what it will cover and concludes with a few thought-provoking questions and a summary. The questions are not exercises in the school textbook sense, but rather things to mull over in your mind or perhaps to research on the Web or in a library. A few ideas for further experimentation are scattered through the text and some are featured in Appendix C, in a discussion of potential projects.

How the Book Is Structured

The book includes four sections:

Section 1 Introduction
Section 1 provides introductory material about this book and the concepts, history, and theory of programming.

Section 2 Programming Fundamentals
Section 2 incorporates the meat of the book. It covers the four basic constructs of programming: sequences, loops, branches, and modules. It also looks at data, operations, and other essential topics. It is designed to be read in sequence.

Section 3 Advanced Topics
Unlike Section 2, Section 3 contains a number of more or less unrelated topics. Its chapters can be read in any order, although the later ones refer back to topics covered earlier. They all assume you have understood the concepts presented in Section 2.

Section 4 Case Studies

This section comprises step-by-step accounts of the development of a document grammar measurement tool and a games framework. It includes some mistakes and describes the backtracking required to fix them. It concludes by showing how the original command-line programs can be turned into easy-to-use graphical user interface (GUI)–based tools. The size of the projects matches what you might expect someone who had completed the book to be capable of tackling on his or her own. The final programs are only for fun, but should help you later create something that is genuinely useful.

Appendices

Appendix A covers the installation of Python and a quick-start guide to using the IDLE programming environment. Appendix B offers a brief guide to some other languages of interest. Appendix C lists books and other resources to further your knowledge and expertise. A glossary of computing terms rounds out the book.

Chapter

2

What Do I Need?

What will we cover?

- *The character and mindset of a programmer*

- *The programming environments used in this book*

The Human Aspects of Programming

Before we go into the technical aspects of this book, I'd like to spend just a few moments on the human side of the activity. My friends often ask me, What do you enjoy about your job? What is it like to write computer programs? It is—or can be—a joyous experience. It really is a lot of fun when an idea, a concept that existed only in your mind's eye, is transformed first into words and symbols on a PC and then into an executing program carrying out the task as intended. The only other activity that gives me anything like the same satisfaction is watercolor painting. In fact, there are many similarities between the two. Both start off as blank sheets, and both require a great deal of preparatory work that to an onlooker gives no clue as to the end result. And both, when completed successfully, are expressions of technical skill as well as artistic creativity.

So what does it take to be a good programmer? The most useful attribute is the right *mindset* to write programs—that is, an innate *curiosity* about things, coupled to a *logical way of thinking* and the *patience* to deal with minute details. These characteristics are all essential requirements for a successful programmer.

The curiosity factor comes into play in looking for answers to problems and being willing to dig around in sometimes obscure documents and help files for the ideas and information needed to complete a task. It also means having a willingness to experiment, to try things out "just to see what happens." Often, these experiments will solve a problem that would otherwise take days of mental anguish and research to resolve. Every programming language has its own syntax and rules that must be obeyed in excruciating detail or your program simply will not work. A programmer must have the patience to check and understand the precise set of rules required to solve the problem at hand and to translate these rules into the programming language being used.

Logical thinking comes into play because computers are intrinsically stupid. They can't really do much except add single digits together and move data from one place to another. Luckily for us, some talented programmers have written programs to hide this basic stupidity. Of course, as a programmer you may well get into a situation where you have to face that stupidity in its raw state. At that point, you have to think for the computer. You have to figure out exactly what needs to be done to your data and when. Remember—computers, being stupid, do so little that they can't make mistakes. Instead, it's we programmers who do that.

Prerequisites

So much for the philosophy! What are the prerequisites for completing this book and being able to write useful programs at the end of it? In principle, you don't *need* anything to understand this book. That is, you could read right through it and ideally understand all of the concepts and examples just from the descriptions given. To get the most from the material, however, I strongly recommend that you follow along, typing in the examples by hand or, if that's too much work, copying the sample code from the CD-ROM into your text editor.[1] You can then run the programs and see the results. To do so, you need to have Python installed on your system as described in Appendix A.

---

1. *Only the longer programs appear on the CD-ROM. In most cases, it's just as fast to type in the short examples as it would be to copy them from a CD!*

Python

Python version 1.5.2 is the latest release at the time of writing and is included on the CD-ROM. The master Web site for Python is:

    http://www.python.org/

You can always find the latest versions there for free downloading. Instructions for installing Python under Windows are given in Appendix A. Python is available on most Linux distributions, and the Python site contains versions or links to versions for most popular operating systems.

Points to Remember

You need logical thinking, curiosity, and patience to program.

Python is freely available for most platforms.

Chapter

3

What Is Programming?

What will we cover?

- *An introduction to the terminology of computing*

- *Some history*

- *A brief look at the structure of a computer program*

A Definition

Computer programming is the art of making a computer do exactly what you want it to do. At the very simplest level, it involves issuing a sequence of commands to a computer to achieve an objective. In the old Microsoft world of MS-DOS,[1] users created text files with lists of commands called *batch files* with a file extension of .BAT. These files simply executed the sequence of commands one after the other as a *batch job*—hence the name.

For example, imagine that you are producing a document (such as this book) that comprises many separate files. Let's assume that your word processor produces backup copies of each file as it saves a new version. At the end of the day you want to put the current version of the document (the latest files)

---

1. *You can still produce batch files in Windows environments today, but in practice they are rarely used. With Windows 98 and Windows 2000, they have been largely superseded by Windows Script Host, which provides a more comprehensive programming capability.*

into a "backup" directory/folder. Finally, to tidy up, you'd like to delete all of the backup files so that you will be ready to start work the next day. A simple batch file to do this would be

```
COPY *.DOC BACKUP
DEL *.BAK
```

If the file were called `SAVE.BAT`, then at the end of each day you could simply type `SAVE` at an MS-DOS prompt. The files would then be saved and the backups deleted. This is a program.

Batch Files on UNIX

Users of UNIX/Linux (and most other operating systems) have their own versions of these files, which are often known as shell scripts. UNIX shell scripts are much more powerful than DOS BAT files, and they support most of the programming techniques that we will be discussing in this book.

If you were a little daunted by that discussion, don't worry. A computer program is simply a sequence of instructions telling the computer how to perform a particular task. It's rather like a recipe: a set of instructions to tell a cook how to make a particular dish. It describes the ingredients (the data) and the sequence of steps (the process) needed to convert the ingredients into a cake or whatever. Programs are very similar in concept.

A Little History

Just as you speak to a friend in a language, so you "speak" to the computer in a language. The only language that the computer understands is called *binary*. Several dialects of this language exist—which is why that cool iMac program won't run on your PC, and vice versa. Binary is very difficult for humans to read or write, so we must instead use an intermediate language that is later translated into binary. This process is rather like watching two heads of state talking at a summit meeting: one speaks, then an interpreter repeats what has been said in Russian, for example. The other head of state replies and the interpreter again repeats the sentence, this time in English.

Just as you usually need a different interpreter to translate English into Russian than the interpreter who translates Arabic into Russian, so you need a different computer translator to convert Python into binary than the one that converts Java into binary.

The very first programmers actually had to enter the binary codes themselves. This process, which is known as *machine code programming*, is incredibly difficult and extremely error-prone. The next step was to create a translator that simply converted English equivalents of the binary codes into binary. Thus, instead of having to remember that the code 001273 05 04 meant add 5 to 4, programmers could simply write ADD 5 4. This very simple improvement made programming much easier. These systems of codes—known as assembler languages—were really the first programming languages, with one existing for each type of computer. *Assembler programming* is still used for a few specialized programming tasks today.[2]

Assembler programming was still very primitive. It simply told the computer what to do at the hardware level—move bytes from this memory location to that memory location, add this byte to that byte, and so on. It remained very difficult, with much programming effort required to perform even simple tasks.

Gradually, computer scientists developed higher-level computer languages to make the job easier. This was just as well, because at the same time users were inventing ever more complex jobs for computers to solve! This competition between computer scientists and users continues today, with new languages appearing to serve evolving needs. This evolution makes programming interesting but also means that any programmer must understand the concepts of programming as well as the specifics of using any particular language.

We'll discuss some of those common concepts next. As we go through the book, we will keep coming back to them, too.

The Common Features of All Programs

A long time ago,[3] a man called Edsgar Dijkstra came up with a concept called *structured programming*. This concept said that all programs can be structured using combinations of four constructs: sequences of instructions, branches, loops, and modules.

Sequences of Instructions
A sequence is the simplest construct, where one instruction follows another (Figure 3-1). The MS-DOS batch file we saw earlier was a simple sequence.

Figure 3-1
Sequence of
instructions

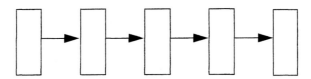

---

2. There are three main areas where you may come across assembler: (1) When writing device drivers for new hardware such as video cards; (2) where program memory size is important—assembler gives the smallest possible programs; and (3) where execution speed must be as fast as possible. Even in the latter case, most of the program is likely to be written in a higher-level language and only the most critical segments written in assembler.
3. Around 1965, actually—but in computing terms, that's almost in the Stone Age.

Branches

Branches occur when the program flow divides into two or more separate streams (Figure 3-2). The actual flow will progress down one of the possible streams depending on whether some test condition is true. This construct is often called a *conditional* construct because of this feature. Branches are the decision-making parts of our programs and provide the computer with an illusion of intelligence. Without branching constructs, programs would simply repeat exactly the same sequence of instructions every time they ran, which would be very boring.

Figure 3-2
Branches

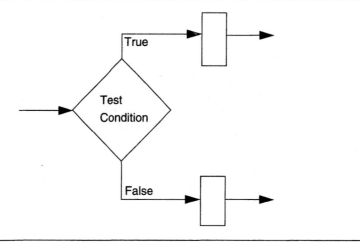

Loops

The loop construct repeats an instruction or sequence of instructions several times (Figure 3-3). Usually, the frequency of the repetition is controlled by a counter value or a test, such as whether the end of a file has been reached. This construct permits programs to handle large volumes of work without restarting each time a new task begins. It also saves a huge amount of effort by the programmer, as the repeated sequence of instructions needs to be written only once. The loop can be thought of as a branch construct where one of the branches jumps back to an earlier point in the program.

Figure 3-3
Loop

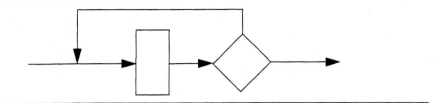

Modules

Modules[4] are a way of wrapping several operations—which may consist of any or several of the other three constructs—into a reusable component. The component can then be used as a "black box" that provides some kind of service to the rest of the program. By turning them into a component, the operations can be easily reused in several places within the program and even in several different programs.

Other Necessary Constituents

Along with these control structures, programs need a few more features to make them useful:

- Data (numbers, characters, dates, and so on)

- Operations (add, subtract, compare, and so on)

- Input/output capability (for example, to display results)

Once you understand those concepts and the way in which a particular programming language implements them, then you can write a program in that language.

Clarifying Some Terminology

We have already said that programming is the art of making a computer do what you want. But what is "a program"?

In practice, two distinct concepts of a program exist. The first concept is the one perceived by the user—an executable file that is installed and can be run as often as needed to perform a task. For example, users speak of running their "word processor program."

---

4. Dijkstra did not actually include modules in his original proposal as they are not an essential construct for writing programs. Nonetheless, modules have been accepted as part of the discipline of programming for many years.

The second concept is the program as seen by the programmer—that is, the text file of instructions to the computer, written in some programming language, that can be translated into an executable file. When you talk about "a program," you should always be clear about which concept you mean.

A programmer writes a program in a *high-level language*, which is then translated into the bits and bytes that the computer understands. In technical speak, the programmer generates *source code* and the translator generates *object code*. Sometimes object code has other names, such as: *P-code, byte code, binary code,* or *machine code.*

The translator can have either of two names: *interpreter* or *compiler.* These terms refer to different techniques of generating object code from source code. In the past, compilers produced object code that could be run on its own (an *executable file*), whereas an interpreter had to be present to run its program. The difference between these terms is blurring today, however, as some compilers now require an interpreter to be present to do a final conversion and some interpreters simply compile their source code into temporary object code and then execute it. Python is an example of the latter type of interpreter. When source code is executed via an interpreter, then the term *scripting* is sometimes used instead of "programming."

From our perspective, none of these fairly subtle variations in terminology makes any real difference. We will simply write source code and use a tool to allow the computer to read and execute it. The terms are introduced here to enable you to understand what other programmers mean if you ask questions on the Internet or on a mailing list.

The Python execution environment can be illustrated as shown in Figure 3-4. The program source code is read by the Python execution environment, which interprets the text and translates it into byte code. The byte code is stored for future use and the translated source code is executed, resulting in interaction with the computer components: display, keyboard/mouse, and data storage. Other Python modules are imported as required.

Figure 3-4
Python
execution
environment

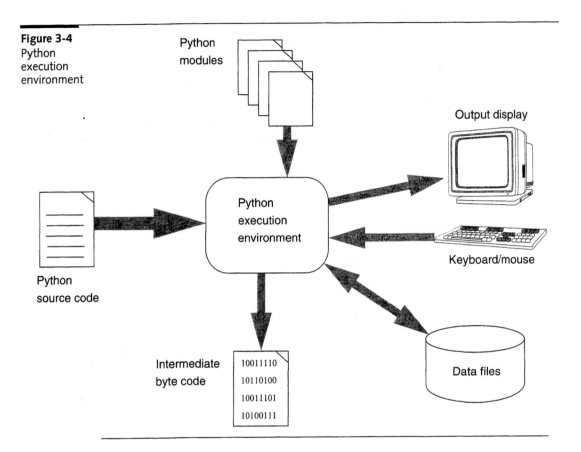

One final piece of terminology that you may encounter is the distinction drawn between *runtime* events and *compile time* events—usually errors. Not surprisingly, these terms indicate the phase of the process when the error occurs. If the error happens during the translation process, it is known as a *compile-time* error and usually indicates a fault in the program source code. If the problem arises after translation, it is known as a *runtime* problem and may lie in the source code, data or execution environment.

The Structure of a Program

The exact structure of a program depends on the programming language and the environment in which you run it. Some general principles apply, however. The first is that all programs must contain two elements: data definitions and statements.

Data Definitions. Most programs operate on data. Therefore, somewhere in the source code, we need to define exactly what type of data is used: numbers, characters, dates, and so on. Different languages handle this requirement very differently. Python allows us to create a new data definition just by using the data. You'll see what I mean in Section 2.

Statements. Statements form the core of your program. They actually manipulate the data we define, do the calculations, print the output, and perform other tasks. The statements of the program can be further classified into three categories:

- *Initialization.* Statements that prepare the program for its main function—perhaps opening a file or logging on to a database or remote network server or just setting up some default values.

- *Core functionality.* The statements that do whatever the program is supposed to do. Drawing to the screen, interacting with the user, fetching and saving data, and performing calculations are all typical program operations that could implement core functionality.

- *Finalization.* Tidying up after the program has done its job, closing files and network connections, writing audit entries, and so on.

Most programs follow one of two structures: batch or event-driven.

Figure 3-5
Structure of a
batch program

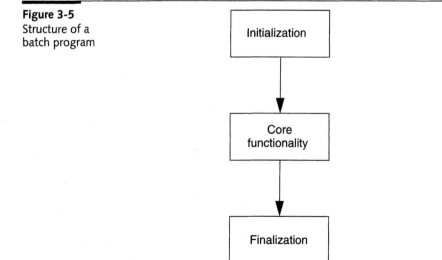

Batch Programs

Batch programs are typically started from a command line (or automatically via a scheduler utility) and tend to follow the pattern shown in Figure 3-5. Some batch programs interact with the user by presenting prompts or text-based menus and then reacting to the users responses. Nevertheless, the flow of control within the program remains internal and so the structure can still be termed batch-oriented.

Event-Driven Programs

Most GUI systems (and embedded control systems, as in your microwave or camera) are event-driven. That is, the operating system sends events to the program, and the program responds to these events as they arrive. Events can include things a user does—like clicking the mouse or pressing a key— or things that the system itself does—like updating the clock or refreshing the screen.

Event-driven programs generally have the structure depicted in Figure 3-6. After initialization, control passes from the program itself to the event generator (usually part of the operating system). It returns to the program only on

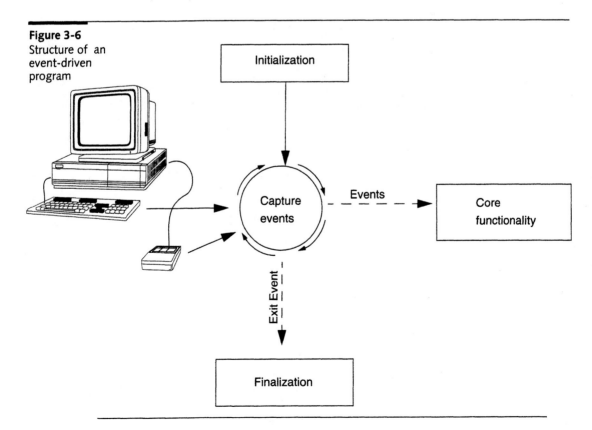

Figure 3-6
Structure of an event-driven program

Initialization

Capture events

Events

Core functionality

Exit Event

Finalization

Things to Ponder

Given what you now know about the nature of programming, have you ever written a program without realizing it? Maybe an MS-DOS batch file or an application macro?

The programming constructs described in this chapter are reminiscent of flowcharts. Does this similarity mean that flowcharts could be used to describe or design a program?

Programmers often refer to their own personal style of working as being either batch mode or event (or interrupt)-driven. Which mode describes the way you organize things in your life?

receipt of an event that indicates the program should exit. Otherwise, the program will remain waiting for and responding to new events forever.

All of the programs we write in the early stages of this book will be batch-oriented. In Section 3, we will take a closer look at event-driven programs. In Section 4, the case studies will demonstrate how batch-oriented programs can be turned into event-driven programs—the opposite transformation is rarely required.

Points to Remember

Programs control the computer.

Programming languages allow us to "speak" to the computer at a level that is closer to how humans think than to how computers "think."

Programs operate on data.

Programs can be either batch-oriented or event-driven.

Chapter
4

Getting Started

What will we cover?

- *Installing Python*
- *Reading Python error messages*

Before we get down to the nitty gritty of writing programs, we need to make sure that our programming environment is installed and working.

Using Python

The exercises in Section 2 assume that you have a properly installed version of Python on your computer. If you do not, go to Appendix A and follow the instructions for installing it on your PC. At the Start|Run dialog, type

```
python
```

The Python interactive prompt should appear inside an MS-DOS session, displaying a message like the following:

```
Python 1.5.2 (#0, Apr 13 1999, 10:51:12) [MSC 32 bit (Intel)]
on win32
Copyright 1991-1995 Stichting Mathematisch Centrum, Amsterdam
>>>
```

You can now type Python commands into the computer and they will be executed by the Python interpreter.

To exit from Python, type CTRL-Z in DOS or CTRL-D in Linux/UNIX.

If you prefer, you can type the Python commands into a text file—say, prog.py—and execute the commands by typing:

```
C:\> python prog.py
```

at the MS-DOS command prompt. This approach is the normal way to execute Python scripts[1] when you aren't just experimenting with an idea.

Running Programs Under Linux/UNIX

Under a UNIX-type operating system, you can use a special trick to make it easier to run your programs. If you create a text file—say, foo.py—containing a Python program, make the first line of the file contain the line:

```
#! /usr/bin/python
```

and make the file executable

```
$ chmod +x foo.py
```

then you can execute your Python program by typing the name of your file just as if it was any other executable program (in fact, you don't even need the .py extension; it just helps you remember that it is a Python file). Obviously, if Python is not in /usr/bin on your system, you will need to substitute the correct location. This shortcut is known as the "shebang" trick in UNIX circles.

You can get help about any of the Python commands that we discuss (as well as many more that we won't cover) in the documentation that comes with Python. Simply navigate to the folder in which Python is installed, change to the Docs folder, and open index.html in your favorite browser. From here

---

1. *In fact you can double-click on the file icon in Explorer and Windows will call Python for you, provided the correct file associations are set up (which the installer should do for you).*

you can visit the Language Reference, Library Reference, or the official Python Tutorial. You will likely find the documentation useful when considering some of the "Things to Ponder" questions at the end of each chapter.

A Word about Python Error Messages

If you type in the commands as we go through them, then sooner or later you will get an error message. It might look something like this:

```
>>> print 'fred' + 7
Traceback (innermost last):
  File "<stdin>", line 1, in ?
TypeError: illegal argument type for built-in operation
```

Don't worry about the exact meaning here, but rather look at the structure.

- The ">>> print ..." line is the erroneous command typed in.

The next two lines describe where the error occurred:

- The "line 1 in ?" means line 1 in the command typed in. If the error occurred in a longer program stored in a source file the "?" would be replaced by the file name.

- The "TypeError..." line indicates what the interpreter thinks is wrong. Sometimes a caret character(^) will point to the part of the line that Python thinks is at fault.[2] Unfortunately, this latter bit of information will often be wrong—remember, computers are dumb! Try looking at the stuff just before the alleged error, even the line (or two!) above.

Use the error information to figure out what's happening. Remember that you are more likely to be at fault than the computer is. Remember, too, that computers are dumb. Probably you just mistyped something or forgot a quote sign or something similar. One common "gotcha" is that Python is *case-sensitive*. That is, spam and Spam are two different words as far as Python is concerned. Remember to check the capitalization when errors strike!

---

2. *Technically, the caret points at the first part of the program that the Python interpreter couldn't understand. That is why the real error may be some way behind the caret symbol.*

In case you were wondering, the mistake in the preceding code was my attempt to add a number to a character string. You're not allowed to do that, so Python objected and indicated the presence of a `TypeError`. You'll discover what a *Type* is when we get to Chapter 6.

▌Points to Remember ▌

You can program Python from the interactive prompt or by typing the program into a text file.

Python documentation exists in HTML format within the Docs *subfolder of the Python installation.*

Error messages may seem cryptic, but they do contain useful information. Study them carefully.

Section 2
Programming Fundamentals

In this section, we look at the four fundamental constructs of programming. We also consider the kinds of data we can use and the operations that we can perform on that data. Other important considerations include how to communicate with our users, how to work with files, and how to catch and respond to errors.

Chapter

5

Simple Sequences

What will we cover?

- *Printing letters and numbers*

- *Describing what we are doing*

- *Extending Python's capabilities*

- *Quitting Python*

Single Statements

A simple sequence of instructions is the most basic program you can write. The simplest sequence is one containing a single command. We will try out some of these sequences here. The bold text in the code describes what you should type at the ">>>" Python prompt; the paragraph following the code explains what happens.

```
>>> print 'Hello there!'
Hello there!
```

The print command makes Python display its results to you. In this case, it prints the sequence of characters H,e,l,l,o,(space),t,h,e,r,e,!. Such a sequence of characters is known in programming circles as a *string of characters*, a *character string*, or just a *string*.

You signify a string by surrounding it with quotes. You can use either single quotes (as in the example) or double quotes (as in "a string"). This approach allows you to include one type of quote within a string that is surrounded by the other type, which is useful for apostrophes:

```
>>> print "Monty Python's Flying Circus has a ' within it..."
Monty Python's Flying Circus has a ' within it
```

Python as a Calculator

You can print more than strings, of course.

```
>>> print 6 + 5
11
```

Here we have printed the result of an *arithmetic operation*—we added 6 and 5. Python recognized the numbers as being numbers, along with the plus sign, and did the sum for us. It then printed the result. So straight away you have a use for Python: it's a handy "pocket calculator"! Try a few more sums.

Other arithmetic operators exist as well:

```
Subtract (-)
Multiply (*)
Divide (/)
```

Using parentheses, you can combine multiple expressions, as in the following command:

```
>>> print ((8 * 4) + (7 - 3)) / (2 + 4)
6
```

Notice the way parentheses were used to group the numbers together. What happens if you type the same sequence without the parentheses? You get the answer 42! That's because Python will evaluate the multiplication and division operators before the addition and subtraction operator. Although you might expect this result mathematically speaking, it may not be what you expect as a programmer! All programming languages have a set of rules to determine the sequence of evaluation of operations, which is known as *operator* precedence. Look at the reference documentation for each language you use to see how operator precedence works for that language. With Python it's usually what logic and intuition would suggest, but occasionally it won't be... As a general rule, it's safest to include the parentheses to ensure that you get what you want in terms of operator precedence when dealing with long series of operations.

Now let's consider another simple sequence:

```
>>> print 15/4
3
```

This command results in a whole number (*integer*) result (that is, 3). Python sees that the numbers are whole numbers and assumes you want to keep them that way. If you want decimal fractions as a result, simply write either the numerator or denominator as a decimal:

```
>>> print 15/4.0
3.75
```

Python will see the 4.0 and realize that we are happy dealing with fractions, which are known as *real numbers* (*floating point*, in computing parlance) so it responds with a fractional result. If you want to stick with whole numbers, you can find the remainder of a division by using the *modulo operator* (which is the % sign in Python) just like a division operator. Python will then print the remainder:

```
>>> print 7/2
3
>>> print 7%2
1
>>> print 7%4
3
```

Experiment with this operator and you will soon get the idea.

Using Format Strings

```
>>>print 'The total is: ', 23+45
The total is: 68
```

You've seen that we can print strings and numbers. Now we have combined the two in one print statement, separating them with a comma. We can extend this feature by using it with a Python trick for displaying data called a format string:

```
>>> print "The sum of %d and %d is: %d" % (7,18,7+18)
The sum of 7 and 18 is: 25
```

In this command the format string contains "%" markers within it. The letter "d" after the % tells Python that a "decimal number" should be placed there. The values to fill in the markers come from the values inside the parentheses following the % sign. Several other letters can also be placed after % markers:

%s	String
%x	Hexadecimal number
%0.2f[1]	A real number with two figures following the decimal point
%4d	Use leading spaces to pad the number out to at least four digits
%04d	Use leading 0's to pad the number out to at least four digits

Several more markers are available as well. The Python documentation provides a complete list (but see the sidebar first).

String Format Codes

The underlying core of Python is written in C, and Python uses the same string formatting conventions as used in C's `printf()` function. This borrowing is quite common in modern programming languages, including C++, Perl, and Tcl.

Python's documentation of the format codes is not easy to find. Look in the Python Library Reference in Section 2.1.5.1 under "More String Operations." The best way of becoming familiar with the use of these codes is simply to experiment by typing examples at the Python interactive prompt and looking at the output.

For example, to try out the floating-point options mentioned in the main text, try the following commands:
```
>>> print "%0.2f" % 123.456
123.46
>>> print "%0.2f" % 123.4
123.40
>>> print "%0.7f" % 123.456
123.4560000
>>> print "%9.2f" % 123.456
   123.46
```

---

1. *The 0 in* %0.2f *is optional; I included it to aid visibility. Without the zero, it can be difficult to spot the decimal point. The figure before the decimal point indicates the minimum number of characters used to print the result. For floating-point operations, it has an effect only if it is larger than the precision specifier plus the whole number part. For an integer value, there is only a single value giving the minimum width.*

Notice that the last example puts three spaces in front of the result. This reflects the fact that we asked for a total of at least nine characters but the actual number requires only six because we also requested that it be rounded to two decimal places.

You can print any Python object with the `print` command. Sometimes the result will not be what you hoped for (perhaps just a description of the kind of object), but you can always print it and Python will do its best to produce something meaningful.

Comments

```
>>> # print "Nothing"
```

You may have expected this statement to print the word "Nothing"; in fact, nothing appeared. Why? Python ignores anything after (and including) a "#" sign, because is is considered a *comment*. Comments represent one way to add annotations to your programs to let you know what's going on. While single-line commands, like those we've been entering, may be easy to understand, as your programs get bigger, comments become an invaluable way of keeping your sanity!

```
>>> print "You can see me" # But you don't see this
You can see me
```

Here the comment appears at the end of a line of code that does execute. The execution ignores the commented part, however.

We'll revisit comments later and see several ways to use them. For now, comments will occasionally appear in our examples just to clarify things. Remember—Python ignores everything from the "#" to the end of the line.

Accessing Modules

```
>>>import sys
```

This command is a strange one. It apparently does nothing. In reality, that's not true. To understand what happened, we need to look at Python's architecture. When you start Python, a bunch of commands are already available to you. They are called *built-ins*, because they are built in to the Python core. Python can also extend the list of commands available by incorporating extension *modules*. The process is a bit like buying a new tool in your favorite hardware store and adding it to your toolbox. The tool is the `sys` part, and the import operation adds it to the toolbox.

The import command makes available an entire set of new modules in the shape of the Python library. Each module, in turn, contains a set of related commands. In this way, Python can be extended to do all sorts of clever things that are not covered in the core system. You can even create, import, and use your own modules, just like the modules provided with Python when you installed it. We'll see how to do that in a later chapter.

So how do we use these new tools?

```
>>> sys.exit()
```

Whoops! What happened there? We executed the exit command defined in the sys module. That command causes Python to exit.[2] Notice that exit is followed by parentheses. That's because exit is a special kind of command, known as a *function*, defined in sys. When we call a Python function we need to supply the parentheses even if there's nothing inside them! We'll look at functions in much more detail later.

Try typing sys.exit without the parentheses. Python responds by telling you that exit is a function rather than by executing it.

Finally, notice that the last two commands are useful only in combination. That is, to exit from Python other than by typing EOF, you need to type

```
>>> import sys
>>> sys.exit()
```

This sequence includes two commands! Now we're getting closer to real programming.... But first we need to talk about data.

Points to Remember

A single command is the simplest program.

We can use Python as a calculator.

To get a fractional result, you must use a floating-point number somewhere in the calculation.

You can create complex output with format strings.

Import modules to access additional facilities.

Exit Python by typing the EOF key combination or programmatically by calling sys.exit( ).

---

2. *Recall that you normally exit Python by typing the end of file (EOF) character at the prompt:* CTRL-Z *on MS-DOS/Windows or* CTRL-D *on UNIX.*

Chapter

6

The Raw Materials

What will we cover?

- *What data is*

- *What variables are*

- *Data types and what to do with them*

- *Defining our own data types*

In any creative activity, we need three basic ingredients: tools, materials, and techniques. For example, when I paint, my tools are my brushes, pencils, and palettes. My techniques are things like washes, wet on wet, blending, and spraying. My materials are the paints, paper, and water. Similarly, when I program, my tools are the programming languages, operating systems, and hardware. My techniques are the programming constructs that we discussed in Chapter 3, my material is the data that I manipulate. In this chapter, we look at the materials of programming.

This chapter is quite long and perhaps a bit dry. The good news is that you don't need to read it all at once. We begin by looking at the most basic types available, then consider how to handle collections of items, and finally look at some more advanced material. You can drop out of the chapter after the collections material, if desired, cover a couple of the following chapters, and then return to this one as we start to use the more advanced bits.

Data: A Definition

Data is one of those terms that everyone uses but few really understand. My dictionary defines it as follows:

> Facts or figures from which conclusions can be inferred; information

That's not too much help but at least gives us a starting point. Let's see if we can clarify things by looking at how "data" is used in programming terms. Data is[1] the "stuff," or raw information, that your program manipulates. Without data a program cannot perform any useful function. Programs manipulate data in many ways, often depending on the *type* of the data. Each data type is also associated with a number of *operations*—things that you can do to it. For example, we can add numbers together. Addition is an operation on the number type of data. Data comes in many types, and we'll look at the most common types and the operations available for those types later.

Variables: A Definition

Data is stored in the memory of your computer. You can liken this situation to the big wall full of boxes used in mailrooms to sort the mail. You can put a letter in any box. Unless each box is labeled with the destination address, this effort is really meaningless. Variables are the labels on the boxes in your computer's memory.

Knowing what data looks like is fine so far as it goes. To manipulate it, however, we need to be able to access it—and that's what variables are used for. In programming terms, we can create *instances* of data types and assign them to *variables*. A variable is a *reference* to a specific area somewhere in the computer's memory. These areas hold the data. In some computer languages, a variable must match the *type* of data to which it points. Any attempt to assign the wrong type of data to such a variable will cause an error. Some programmers prefer this type of system, which is known as *static typing*, because it can prevent some subtle errors that can prove difficult to detect.

---

1. *Language purists will point out that* data *is the plural form of* datum *and therefore should use plural verbs. Most people don't do that and I will follow the common usage. Language purists can, of course, change my faulty grammar in their own copies of the book!*

In Python a variable takes and retains the type of the data assigned to it. You will receive a warning if you try to mix data in strange ways—for example, by adding a string to a number. (Recall the example error message in Chapter 4? It involved just that kind of error.) We can change the type of data to which a variable points by reassigning the variable.

```
>>> q = 7      # q is now a number
>>> print q
7
>>> q = "Seven"     # reassign q to a string
>>> print q
Seven
```

Note that q was set to point to the number 7 initially. It maintained that value until we made it point at the character string "Seven". Thus Python variables maintain the type of the item to which they point, but we can change the item to which they point simply by reassigning the variable. The original data is then "lost" and Python will erase it from memory (unless another variable points at it, too) in a process known as *garbage collection.*

Garbage collection can be likened to the mailroom clerk who comes around occasionally and removes any packages that are in boxes with no labels. If he can't find an owner or address on the packages, he throws them in the garbage.

Let's look at some examples of data types and see how all of this information fits together.

Primitive Data Types

Primitive data types are so named because they are the most basic types of data we can manipulate. More complex data types are really combinations of the primitive types. The primitive types are the building blocks upon which all the other types are built—indeed, they form the very foundation of computing. They include letters, numbers, and something called a *Boolean* type. Let's see what they look like.

Character Strings

We encountered character strings in Chapter 5, where we saw that they are any sequence of characters that can be printed on your screen. (In fact, some nonprintable control characters exist as well.) In Python, strings can be represented in several ways.

With single quotes:

```
>>> print 'Here is a string'
Here is a string
```

With double quotes:

```
>>> print "Here is a very similar string"
Here is a very similar string
```

With triple double quotes:

```
>>> print """ Here is a very long string that can
if we wish span several lines and Python will
preserve the lines as we type them..."""
Here is a very long string that can
if we wish span several lines and Python will
preserve the lines as we type them...
```

One special use of strings is to build in documentation for Python functions that we create ourselves. We'll see this use later in the book.

You can access the individual characters in a string by treating the string as an *array* of characters (as discussed in "Other Collection Types" later in this chapter). The programming language usually provides some operations to help you manipulate strings—find a substring, join two strings, copy one string to another, and so on. In Python these operations are provided by the string module, which we'll discuss in more detail later. Python also includes some built-in string operations.

String Operators

A number of operations can be performed on strings. Some are built in to Python, and many others are provided by modules that you must import (as we did with sys in Chapter 5). Table 6-1 lists two string operators. We can see these operators in action in the following examples:

```
>>> print 'Again and ' + 'again' # string concatenation
Again and again
>>> print 'Repeat ' * 3                    # string repetition
Repeat Repeat Repeat
>>> print 'Again ' + ('and again ' * 3) # combine '+' and '*'
Again and again and again and again
```

We can also assign character strings to variables:

```
>>> s1 = 'Again '
>>> s2 = 'and again '
>>> print s1 + (s2 * 3)
Again and again and again and again
```

Notice that the last two examples produced the same output.

	Operator	Description
Table 6-1 String Operators	S1 + S2	Concatenation of S1 and S2
	S1 * N	N repetitions of S1

Integers

Integers are whole numbers that range from a large negative value through to a large positive value. The limitations are important to remember. Normally, we don't think of numbers as being restricted in size; but on a computer, however, upper and lower limits apply. The size of this upper limit is known as MAXINT and depends on the number of bits used on your computer to represent a number. On most current computers, it's 32 bits; hence MAXINT is appoximately 2 billion.[2] Numbers with positive and negative values are known as *signed integers*. You can also use *unsigned integers*, which are

---

2. *MAXINT is the largest number that can be stored in the internal word format of the computer. A 32-bit processor can store 32 binary digits, or bits; thus MAXINT is 2^{31}. On a 16-bit processor, it would be 2^{15} or 32767.*

restricted to positive numbers, including zero. A 32-bit computer can therefore have a larger maximum number available—2 * MAXINT or 4 billion—because we can use the space previously employed for representing negative numbers to represent more positive numbers.

Why is this limitation important? Because integers are restricted in size to MAXINT, if you add two integers together such that their total is greater than MAXINT, then the actual figure returned by the computer may be wildly wrong. On some operating systems and with some languages, the wrong value is returned as is (usually with some kind of special variable or *flag* set so that you can test for an error). In other cases, an error condition is raised; either your program can handle this error or the program will exit. Python generates errors and provides mechanisms to handle those errors if we wish; otherwise, it will terminate the program and generate an `OverflowError` error message:

```
>>> print 2000000000 * 2
Traceback (innermost last):
  File "<pyshell#5>", line 1, in ?
    print 2000000000 * 2
OverflowError: integer multiplication
```

Arithmetic Operators

We've already seen most of the arithmetic operators that you need in Chapter 5. Table 6-2 recaps these operators.

Table 6-2
Arithmetic and Bitwise Operators

Operator Example	Description
M + N	Addition of M and N
M - N	Subtraction of N from M
M * N	Multiplication of M and N
M / N	Division, either integer or floating-point result depending on the types of M and N; if either M or N is a real number, the result will be real
M % N	Modulo: find the remainder of M divided by N
M**N	Exponentiation: M to the power N

We haven't seen the last operator listed in Table 6-2 before, so let's look at an example of creating some integer variables and using the exponentiation operator:

```
>>> i1 = 2    # create an integer and assign it to i1
>>> i2 = 4
>>> i3 = 2**4  # assign the result of 2 to the power 4 to i3
>>> print i3
16
>>> print i1**i2    # the same but using the variables
16
```

Real Numbers (Floating-Point Numbers)

Real numbers (also known as floating-point numbers) include fractions. They can represent very large numbers—much bigger than MAXINT—but with less *precision.*[3] That is, two real numbers that should be identical may not seem to be when the computer compares them to each other. The computer merely approximates some of the lowest details, so 4.0 could be represented by the computer as 3.9999999.... or as 4.000000....01. These approximations are close enough for most purposes, but occasionally they become important.[4] If you get a strange result when using real numbers, bear this limitation in mind. In particular, it's best not to compare two floating-point numbers directly but rather to test whether they are within some limit of each other—perhaps by subtracting or rounding them first.

Floating-point numbers can use the same operators as integers do. They also have the capability to truncate the number to an integer value.

Complex or Imaginary Numbers

If you have a scientific or mathematical background, you may be wondering about *complex numbers.* If that's not your background, then you may not have heard of *imaginary numbers*—and you can safely skip this section. If you are familiar with them, note that some programming languages, including

---

3. If you are familiar with scientific notation in math, whereby 3000 can be represented as 3×10^3, note that the computer stores floating-point numbers in a very similar way. That is, it uses the base value plus the power to which the base must be raised.
4. Financial calculations should never use floating-point numbers because of these inaccuracies. Instead, store financial sums as integers representing the amount in the lowest denomination available, such as cents. You can then perform precise calculations and convert the result into a decimal form for display purposes. Special modules are often available to handle large financial calculations for occasions when plain integers aren't large enough.

Python, provide built-in support for the complex number type. Even those languages that lack this capability usually provide a module of functions for handling complex numbers.

In Python a complex number is represented as follows:

```
(real+imaginaryj)
```

Thus a simple complex number addition looks like the following:

```
>>> M = (2+4j)
>>> N = (7+6j)
>>> print M + N
(9+10j)
```

All of the integer operations also apply to complex numbers.

Boolean Values

The Boolean type has only two possible values: *true* or *false*. Some languages support Boolean[5] values directly, whereas others use a convention whereby some numeric value (often 0) represents false and another (often 1 or -1) represents true.

Boolean values are sometimes known as "truth values" because they are used to test whether something is true. For example, if you write a program to back up all the files in a directory, you might back up each file and then ask the operating system for the name of the next file. If there are no more files to save, the program will return an empty string. You can then test whether the name is an empty string and store the result as a Boolean value (true if it is empty). You'll see how we would use that result later in this book. Table 6-3 lists the Boolean operators.

---

5. The term Boolean comes from a nineteenth-century mathematician named George Boole, who studied logic and laid down the rules of logic known as Boolean algebra.

Table 6-3	Operator Example	Description	Effect
Boolean Operators	A and B	AND	True if A,B are both true; false otherwise.
	A or B	OR	True if *either* or *both* of A,B are true. False if both A and B are false.
	A == B	Equality	True if A is equal to B.
	A != B *or* A <> B	Inequality	True if A is NOT equal to B.
	not B	Negation	True if B is *not true*.

The negation operator acts on a single value, whereas the other Boolean operators all compare two values.

Boolean Expressions

Although we talk about Boolean data types mostly we use Boolean *expressions*. An expression is simply a set of values and operators combined to produce a result. If that result is interpreted as a Boolean value, then we call it a Boolean expression.

Typical Boolean expressions are tests such as

```
len(X) > 10
```

This expression will be true if the length of X is greater than 10 and false if it is less than or equal to 10. Comparison operators are typically used to construct Boolean expressions; these expressions are then often combined using Boolean operators to form even more complex expressions. Boolean expressions are used in both the looping and conditional programming constructs.

Python interprets most values as Boolean values in a fairly logical fashion. For example, numbers are true if the value is anything other than 0. Collections, including strings, are true if they are not empty. Variables used to reference objects are considered true if they reference a valid object and false if the object is None. **None** is a special Python value indicating an invalid object. If you try to use an invalid object you will get an error message, so testing for equality to **None** can prevent such an error.

Collections

Computer science has built an entire discipline around the study of *collections* and their various behaviors. Sometimes collections are called *containers*. In this section, we will look first at the collections supported in Python. We conclude with a brief summary of some other collection types that you might encounter in other languages.

Python Collections

List

A list is a sequence of items (or *elements*). What makes it different from an array is its ability to grow—you just add another item. In most programming languages, however, a list is not usually indexed. Thus, to find the item you need you must step through the list from beginning to end, checking each element to see if it's the right one. Python includes built-in lists that you can index. As we will see, this feature is very useful.

Python provides many operations on collections, nearly all of which apply to lists; a subset applies to other collection types, including strings, which are just a special type of list of characters.[6] To create and access a list in Python, we use square brackets. You can create an empty list by using a pair of square brackets with nothing inside, or you can create a list with contents by separating the values with commas inside the brackets:

```
>>> aList = []
>>> another = [1,2,3]
>>> print another
[1, 2, 3]
```

We can access the individual elements using an index number, where the first element is 0,[7] inside square brackets:

```
>>> print another[2]
3
```

We can also change the values of the elements of a list in a similar fashion:

```
>>> another[2] = 7
>>> print another
[1, 2, 7]
```

You can use negative index numbers to access members from the end of the list. This technique is most commonly seen using -1 to get the last item:

```
>>> print another[-1]
7
```

---

6. *The major difference between strings and lists is that you can't change the values of characters within a string, they are, like tuples, immutable. Unlike with tuples, however, you can append characters to a string using the "+" operator, although the result is actually a new string.*
7. *In computing, number ranges traditionally start from 0, so the first element of list L would be* L[0]*, the second* L[1] *and so on.*

We can also add new elements to the end of a list using the append ( ) operator:[8]

```
>>> aList.append(42)
>>> print aList
[42]
```

We can even hold one list inside another. Lets's append our second list to the first:

```
>>> aList.append(another)
>>> print aList
[42, [1, 2, 7]]
```

The result is a list of two elements, where the second element is itself a list (as shown by the square brackets around it). This operation is useful because it allows us to build up representations of tables or grids using a list of lists. We can then access the element 7 by using a double index:

```
>>> print aList[1][2]
7
```

The first index, 1, extracts the second element, which is itself a list. The second index, 2, extracts the third element of the sublist.

The opposite of adding elements is, of course, removing them. To remove elements, we use the del command:

```
>>> del aList[1]
>>> print aList
[42]
```

If we want to join two lists together, we can use the same concatenation operator (+) that we used with strings:

```
>>> newList = aList + another
>>> print newList
[42, 1, 2, 7]
```

---

8. Technically, *append* is a method of the List object. For now, we will consider it to be just a special type of operator. We'll explain more about object types at the end of this chapter.

In the same way, we can apply the repetition operator to populate a list with multiples of the same value:

```
>>> zeroList = [0] * 5
>>> print zeroList
[0, 0, 0, 0, 0]
```

Finally, we can determine the length of a list by using the built-in len( ) function:

```
>>> print len(aList)
1
>>> print len(zeroList)
5
```

Tuple

Not every language provides a tuple construct, even though it can prove extremely useful. A tuple is really just an arbitrary collection of values that can be treated as a unit. In many ways it is like a list, but with the significant difference that tuples are *immutable*—that is, you can't change them or append to them once they are created. In Python, tuples are represented by parentheses containing a comma-separated list of values. Consider the following example:

```
>>> aTuple = (1,3,5)
>>> print aTuple[1]     # use indexing like a list
3
>> aTuple[2] = 7    # error, can't change a tuple's elements
Traceback (innermost last):
  File "<pyshell#20>", line 1, in ?
      aTuple[2] = 7
TypeError: object doesn't support item assignment
```

The two main points to remember about tuples are as follows:

- While parentheses are used to define the tuple, square brackets are used to index it.

- You can't change a tuple once it is created.

Otherwise, most of the list operations also apply to tuples.

Dictionary or Hash

A dictionary, as the name suggests, contains a value associated with some key, in the same way that a literal dictionary associates a meaning with a word. The value can be retrieved by "indexing" the dictionary with the key. Unlike with a literal dictionary, the key doesn't need to be a character string (although it often is), but can be any immutable type including numbers and tuples. Similarly, the values associated with the keys can be any kind of Python data type. Dictionaries are usually implemented internally using an advanced programming technique known as a hash table.[9] For that reason a dictionary may sometimes be referred to as a *hash*.

Because access to the dictionary values occurs via the key, you can put in only elements with unique keys. Dictionaries are immensely useful structures that are provided as a built-in type in Python. In many other languages, however, you must use a module or even build your own. We can use dictionaries in many ways and we'll see plenty of examples later. For now, let's create a dictionary in Python, fill it with some entries, and read them back:

```
>>> dict = {}
>>> dict['boolean'] = "A value of either true or false"
>>> dict['integer'] = "A whole number"
>>> print dict['boolean']
A value of either true or false
```

Notice that we initialize the dictionary with braces,[10] then use square brackets to assign and read the values.

Because of their internal structure, dictionaries support very few of the collection operators. In particular, none of the concatenation, repetition, or appending operations works. To assist us in accessing the dictionary keys, we can use the keys() function, which returns a list of all keys in a dictionary.

Other Collection Types

You might come across many other specialized types of collection in discussions or in programming books. We won't use any of these types in this book, but we will provide some idea of the most common terms and their meanings.

---

9. One side effect of hashing is that dictionaries do not store their data in any recognizable order. Thus you cannot extract elements in sequence directly, but rather must create a list of the keys, sort them into order, and then use the sorted list to extract the values in the corresponding order.
10. You can initialize the dictionary by using key:value pairs; thus dict = {'list':'a collection'} is equivalent to dict = {}; dict['list'] = 'a collection'.

Array or Vector

An array is a fixed-size list of elements that are indexed for easy and fast retrieval. Usually you have to say up front how many elements you want to store, and sometimes you can change the size. Nevertheless, you must always create the space before you assign any values to the array. In Python arrays are effectively implemented using lists. Strings are often implemented as arrays of characters in programming languages, and Python strings can be envisioned in much the same way, although you can't change them. You can, however, access the individual letters of a string using indexing as with an array or list.

Stack

Think of a stack of trays in a cafeteria-style restaurant. A member of the restaurant staff puts a pile of clean trays on top, and these trays are removed one by one by customers. The trays at the bottom of the stack get used last (and least!).

Data stacks work the same way: you *push* an item onto the stack or *pop* one off. The item popped off is always the last one pushed on. This property of stacks is sometimes called *Last In First Out (LIFO)*.[11] One useful property of stacks is that you can reverse a list of items by pushing the list onto the stack and then popping it off again. The result will be the reverse of the starting list (Figure 6-1).

Stacks are not built into Python. Instead, you must write program code to implement the behavior. Lists are usually the best starting point because, like stacks, they can grow as needed. In Python we can use the `list.append` method and the -1 index trick to add/access the end of a list and the `del` command to remove the popped item.

---

11. *It could just as validly be called First In Last Out (FILO) but this terminology is less commonly seen, perhaps because filo (phyllo) is also a type of pastry!*

Figure 6-1
Reversing a
string using a
stack

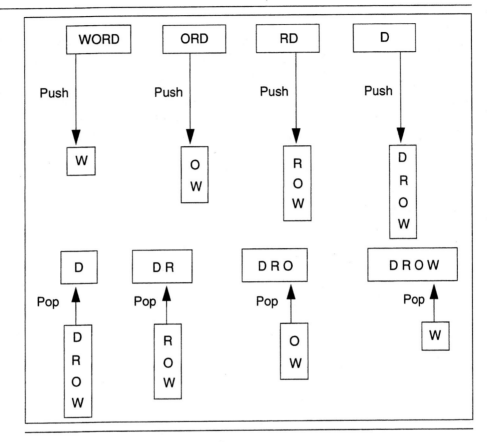

Queue

A queue resembles a stack, except that the first item into a queue is also the first item out. This organization is known as *First In First Out* (FIFO) behavior. Python doesn't directly support queues, so we would need to build them ourselves from lists.

Bag

A bag is a collection of items with no specified order, possibly including duplicates. Bags usually have operators to enable you to add, find, and remove elements. In Python, bags are represented by ordinary lists.

Set

A set has the property of storing only one of each item. You can usually test whether an item appears in a set (membership). You can also add, remove, and retrieve elements and join two sets together in various ways corresponding to set theory in math (for example, union, intersect). Sets can be implemented in Python by using the built-in dictionary or list types.

Many other collection types exist as well, but the types profiled here are the ones that you are most likely to come across in books and articles. In this book we will deal with only the basic Python collection types described earlier, so you can treat this section as a reference for future use.

Advanced Data Types

Files

As a computer user, you know all about files—they form the very basis of nearly everything we do with computers. It should come as no surprise to discover that most programming languages provide a special *file* type of data. Because files and their processing are so important, we will defer our discussion of them until later, when they get an entire chapter (Chapter 12) to themselves.

Dates and Times

Dates and times are often given dedicated types in programming languages. At other times, they are simply represented as large numbers (typically, the number of seconds from some fixed reference date/time, known as the *epoch*). In some cases, the date type is a *complex type*, as described in the next section. This approach usually makes it easier to extract the month, day, hour, or other date/time information. Python supports dates through the time module as described in Chapter 11.

Complex/User-Defined Types

Sometimes the basic types may prove inadequate, even when combined in collections. In that case, we can group several bits of data together and treat the group as a single unit. An example might be the description of an address: a house number, a street name, a town, and a postal ZIP code. Most languages allow us to group such information together in a *record* or *structure*.

In Python, such a structure is called a class:[12]

```
>>> class Address:
        def __init__(self, Hs, St, Town, Zip):
            self.Hs_Number = Hs
            self.Street = St
            self.Town = Town
            self.Zip_Code = Zip
```

The preceding code may look a little arcane, but we'll see what the def __init__(...) and self bits mean in Chapter 17, on object orientation. The main thing is to recognize that we have gathered several pieces of data into a single structure.

Accessing User-Defined Types

We can assign a user-defined data type to a variable, but to access the individual *fields* of the type we must use a special mechanism (which will be defined by the language). Usually this access is achieved by inserting a dot— hence the mechanism is sometimes called the *dot operator*.

Consider the following Python code:

```
>>> addr = Address(7,"High St.","Anytown","12345")
>>> print addr.Hs_Number, addr.Street
7 High St.
```

This code creates an instance of our Address type and assigns it to the variable addr. It then prints out the Hs_Number and Street fields of the newly created instance using the dot operator.

User-Defined Operators

In some languages, user-defined types can have operations defined as well. This capability is the basis of *object-oriented programming*. We dedicate Chapter 17 to this topic. For now, simply note that an object is a collection of data elements and the operations associated with that data, wrapped up as a single unit. Python uses objects extensively in its standard library of modules and allows programmers to create their own object types.

---

12. *If you are typing in this code, note that indentation is very important. Also note that two underscores appear on each side of init.*

Operator Overloading

Some programming languages, including Python, support *operator overloading*— that is, the application of a single operator to different data types. Specifically, you can define your own version of built-in operators for newly defined types.

Some languages (such as Lisp) go still further and allow you to change the existing operators' behavior for the built-in types . Making such a change is usually a very bad idea because the behavior of the program becomes virtually impossible to understand! (Just imagine someone redefining integer addition to do a hard disk format "on the fly"!) Even for types we define ourselves, it is best to overload operators in as meaningful a way as possible.

Object operations are accessed in the same way as data members of a user-defined type (that is, via the dot operator) but otherwise look like functions. These special functions are called *methods*. We have already seen such a function in the append( ) operation of a list. Recall that to use it we must tag the function call onto the variable name:

```
>>> listObject = []     # an empty list
>>> listObject.append(42)   # // method call of List object
>>> print listObject
[42]
```

When an object type, known as a *class*, is provided in a module, we must import the module (as we did with sys earlier), then prefix the object type with the module name to create an instance that we can store in a variable. We can then use the variable without using the module name.

We will illustrate this idea by considering a fictitious module meat, which provides a Spam[13] class. We import the module, create an instance of Spam, and access its operations and data as follows:

```
>>> import meat
>>> mySpam = meat.Spam()   # create instance, use module name
>>> mySpam.slice()             # use a Spam operation
>>> print mySpam.ingredients   # access Spam data
{Pork:40%, Ham:45%, Fat:15%}
```

---

13. Spam *is a common name in Python circles for anything for which we don't have a better name! It comes from a famous Monty Python sketch. Other programming language communities tend to use* foo *for the same purpose.*

Other than the need to create an instance, there's no real difference between using objects provided within modules and functions found within modules. Think of the object name simply as a label that keeps related functions and variables grouped together.

Alternatively, you can think of objects as representing real-world things, to which we as programmers can do things. That view reflects the origins of objects in programs: writing computer simulations of real-world situations.

Python-Specific Operators

This book's primary objective is to teach you to program. Although it uses Python in its examples, there is no reason why, after having read this book, you couldn't use another language instead. Indeed, that's exactly what I expect you to do, because no single programming language can do everything. As a result of that objective, no attempt is made to teach all of the features of Python. Instead, we focus on those features that are generally found in other languages too. There are several Python-specific features that, while quite powerful, are not described here at all, including special operators. Most programming languages have operations that they support but that other languages do not. These "unique" operators often bring new programming languages into being, and they are certainly important factors in determining how popular the language ultimately becomes.

For example, Python supports such relatively uncommon operations as *list slicing* (Spam[X:Y]) and *tuple assignment* (X, Y = 12, 34). It also has the facility to perform an operation on every member of a collection using its map() function. There are so many other features that it's often said that "Python comes with the batteries included." For details of how these Python-specific operations work, consult the Python documentation.

Things to Ponder

Are there other types of data that you think would be useful?

Could you create a user-defined type that would meet your need?

Would this user-defined type have any disadvantages compared to a built-in type?

Finally, it's worth pointing out that some of these "Python-specific" features may also be found in some other languages, although they will not all be found in every language. The operators that we cover in this book are generally available in some form in virtually all modern programming languages.

And that concludes our look at the raw materials of programming. Let's move on to the more exciting topic of techniques and see how we can put these materials to work.

▌ Points to Remember ▐

Data comes in many types, and the operations you can successfully perform will depend on the type of data you are using.

Simple data types include character strings, numbers, and Boolean (or "truth") values.

Unlike real-world numbers, computer numbers have a limited range of sizes.

Complex data types include collections, files, dates, and user-defined data types.

Variables provide a reference to a storage location into which data can be placed.

Some languages, including Python, can store any type of data in a variable.

Some languages allow you to specify the type of data held by a variable, which can help to prevent programming mistakes.

The same operator (for example, "+") may be available for different types, but the results may not be identical or even apparently related!

To use the object types provided in modules, you must first create an instance of the object and then use it to access the required features.

Python provides many more operators than the ones mentioned in this chapter. Consult the Python Reference documents for more information on what's available.

Chapter

7

More Sequences and Other Things

What will we cover?

- *A new way of creating Python programs*

- *The use of variables to store information*

- *Ways to combine a sequence of commands to perform a task*

Now that we know how to type simple single-entry commands into Python and have started to consider the forms and uses of data, let's see what happens when we type multiple commands into Python. You have probably noticed that if you use the Python interactive prompt to enter your programs, there's no way to save your work. This problem is bad enough when you are dealing with short programs. From now on, however, our programs will get longer and it's painful retyping them every time. You have two options[1] to ease the pain:

1. Enter your programs into a text file ending with the extension .py[2]—for example, myprog.py. Next, start an MS-DOS prompt[3] and type

```
C:> python myfile.py
```

---

1. *If you are using Microsoft Windows, you can use Pythonwin, which is downloaded as part of the* winall *package. This package gives access to all Windows MFC low-level programming functions and, importantly, includes a very good alternative to IDLE. Pythonwin only works in Windows, but it's nice to have a choice!*
2. *If you use an editor that supports syntax coloring, such as vim or emacs, then it will also make life easier.*
3. *If you are using Linux or another UNIX variant, then any shell prompt will do.*

where you substitute the name of your program file for `myfile.py`.

2. If you installed Python version 1.5.2, then you also installed a tool called IDLE. Appendix A provides basic instructions for using it. Also read the help file to obtain some brief information on each menu option. The key point to grasp is that you should create a new file window and run your programs via the `Edit|Run` menu.

IDLE offers several advantages over using the MS-DOS interactive prompt or even over using Notepad or other primitive editors:

- Easy cut-and-paste operations

- The ability to cursor up to a previous line and hit `Enter` to create a new editable copy of that line, which saves retyping the line from scratch (this option works only within the Python Shell window)

- Syntax coloring to highlight missed quote signs, keywords, and other significant elements.

From this point forward, the book assumes that you are entering your programs using IDLE. For this reason, the Python >>> prompt won't be shown except in trivial examples for you to try interactively.

Sequences Using Variables

Let's start to put together what we've learned about data, variables, and sequences. Try typing in these examples:

```
>>> v = 7
>>> w = 18
>>> x = v + w     # use our variables in a calculation
>>>print x
25
```

Here we are creating variables (`v`, `w`, `x`) and manipulating them. It's rather like using the "M" button on your pocket calculator to store a result for later use. We can make our output prettier by using a format string to print the result:

```
>>> print "The sum of %d and %d is: %d" % (v,w,x)
The sum of 7 and 18 is: 25
```

One advantage of format strings is that we can store them in variables, too:

```
>>> s = "The sum of %d and %d is: %d"
>>> print s % (v,w,x)
The sum of 7 and 18 is: 25
```

This technique is especially useful if we want to print out a number of tables of data, for example, and would like all of them to have the same layout. Storing the layout format as a variable makes it easy to keep consistency across the tables. If we need to change the layout, we have to change it in only one place, and the changes will be subsequently reflected in all of the tables.

Let's try out some new operators and solve some simple arithmetic problems.

Calculating Areas

Finding the Area of a Circle

We want to find the area of a circle for which we know the radius:

```
# Radius is pi times radius squared.
# We need to use pi, and the exponentiation operator.
import math # defines value of pi among other things
radius = 5
area = math.pi * (radius**2)
print area
```

Finding the Area of a Complex Shape

Figure 7-1 gives the size and shape of a room for which we want to find the area of the floor, perhaps to work out the cost of carpeting. We can use basic arithmetic to calculate the total area by taking the areas of the three rectangles A, B, and C. We know the area of a rectangle is length times breadth, so we can calculate the areas of A and C easily. To calculate B, we need to subtract the combined lengths of A and C from 14 and the short width of A from the long width of A. We can do all of this in Python using the following sequence:

```
# set the known values
totalLength = 14
lenA = 4.8
lenC = 4.1
longA = 8
shortA = 5.2
widthC = 3.9
# Determine B's dimensions
lenB = total Length - (lenA + lenC)
widthB = longA - shortA
```

```
now the area of B
B = lenB * widthB
# So the total area is = A + B + C:
Total = (longA * lenA) + B + (lenC * widthC)
print "The total area is: ", Total
```

Figure 7-1
Example: area
of a room

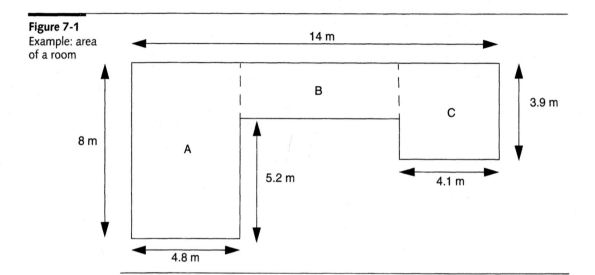

If all has gone well, you should get a result of 68.67. Although you could have solved this problem by using a simple pocket calculator or the Python interactive prompt, saving it as a file allows you to repeat the calculation easily in the future. More importantly, if you have to calculate the area of a different room with different sizes, you need to edit only the top five lines and rerun the program.

Notice also that this example conforms to the classic batch-style program discussed in Chapter 3—we initialize the variables, perform the computation, display the result, and exit. It's our longest program so far by a long way— 15 lines!

The next example will be even simpler mathematically. Nevertheless, we will stick with it over the next few chapters, gradually improving the flexibility of the design as we discover new programming techniques.

The Twelve Times (Multiplication) Table

Do you recall that we can type long strings by enclosing them in triple quotes? Let's use that information to construct a multiplication table:

```
multiplier = 12
s = """
1 x 12 = %d
2 x 12 = %d
3 x 12 = %d
"""        # be careful—you can't put comments inside
           # strings; they'll  become part of the string!
print s % (multiplier, 2 * multiplier, 3 * multiplier)
```

By extending the string and value set, we could print out the full 12 times table from 1 to 12. But that's a lot of typing. Is there a better way? The answer is "yes," and we'll see how in the next chapter.

Things to Ponder

There are quite a few problems that we can solve using just a sequence of steps—it's how most people use pocket calculators after all. Can you think of a common task you perform that could be solved in this way?

Can you think of any uses for comments other than just explaining the code? We'll look at some ideas in Section 3 as well.

Points to Remember

IDLE is a cross-platform development tool for writing Python programs.

Variables can store intermediate results for later use.

Modules can be a source of useful constants (such as pi) as well as services. The math and string modules both provide many examples.

Chapter

8

Looping, or the Art of Repeating Oneself

What will we cover?

- *Ways to use loops to cut down on repetitive typing*

- *Different types of loop and when to use them*

In the last exercise in Chapter 7, we printed out part of the 12 times table. This task took a lot of typing, however, and if we needed to extend the table, it would be very time-consuming. Fortunately, a much better option is available, and it's here that we start to see the real power that programming languages offer us.

FOR Loops

We can use the programming language to do the repetition, by substituting a variable that increases in value each time the code repeats. In Python, the for loop has the following structure:

```
for i in range(1, 13): # Notes 1, 2, 3
    print "%d x 12 = %d" % (i, i*12) # Note 4
```

■ *Note 1:* We need to specify 13 in the `range(1, 13)` part because `range()` generates a list from the first number up to, but not including, the second number. This behavior may seem somewhat bizarre at first, but there are reasons[1] for it and you get used to it.

■ *Note 2:* The `for` loop in Python is actually a `foreach` loop, in that it applies the subsequent code sequence (or *block*) to each member of a collection. In this case, the collection is the list of numbers generated by the Python `range()` function . You can see the list by typing

```
>>> print range(1, 13)
[1, 2, 3, 4, 5, 6, 7, 8, 9, 10, 11, 12]
```

As you see, the result is a list containing the numbers 1 through 12.

■ *Note 3:* You need to type a colon (`:`) at the end of the for clause. It signals Python that the next statement is the body of the `for` loop. The "statement" can be a single statement, in which case it can appear on the same line, like this:

```
>>> for n in [1, 2, 3]: print n
1
2
3
```

Alternatively, it can be a sequence of statements, known as a *block* in programming parlance.

■ *Note 4:* If we place the statement or block under the line containing the `for` clause, it *must* be indented by some arbitrary amount using either spaces or tabs. Python doesn't care how far you indent these lines, but they must all be indented by the same amount. Don't mix tabs and spaces, although you can use either.

WHILE Loops

The `for` loop is not the only type of looping construct available. This flexibilty is just as well, because `for` loops require us to know—or be able to calculate in advance—the number of iterations that we want to perform. But what happens when we want to keep doing a specific task until some event occurs but we

---

1. The `len()` *function returns the number of items in a list, but when indexing we start at 0. Thus the range of indexes is 0 -* `(len-1)`, *which is exactly what the* `range ()` *function gives us when combined with* `len()`: `range(0, len(aList))`.

don't know when that event will take place? For example, we might want to read and process data from a file, but not know in advance how many data items the file contains. We just want to continue processing data until we reach the end of the file. That's possible but difficult in a `for` loop.

To solve this problem, we have another type of loop—the `while` loop. It looks like this in Python:

```
j = 1          # initialize a variable
while j <= 12:   # now test it
    print "%d x 12 = %d" % (j, j*12)
    j = j + 1    # finally increment it
```

Do you see the colon (`:`) at the end of the preceding `while` loop? As with the `for` loop, it tells Python that a chunk of code (a *block*) is coming up. Also, as in the `for` loop, the statements making up the block of code to be repeated must be indented by a uniform amount under the `while` statement.

Indentation versus Block Markers

Python uses indentation to indicate the presence of a block of code. Other programming languages use a special symbol or word to indicate where the block starts and ends. The most common block markers are "begin" and "end" and pairs of braces. Some programmers prefer to use block markers because they make the layout of their code less critical, as the position of the statements on a line no longer matters. Indentation is still a good idea, because it emphasizes the logical structure of the program. You can see some examples of block marking in the other languages described in Appendix B.

In practice most programmers don't find Python's indentation rules difficult to follow because they reflect good programming style. Python doesn't place many restrictions on how much indentation is provided—a single space is sufficient, although most people use three or four spaces or a single tab. The only restriction is that the indentation be consistent within a block.

If you are using IDLE, it will handle most indentation issues for you, automatically detecting when you need to increase indentation and returning you to the previous level at the end of a block when you hit `Delete`. It also provides region indent/unindent features in case you need to move an entire section of code.

Revisiting the Twelve Times (Multiplication) Table

Let's return to our 12 times table. The loop we created works very well for printing out the 12 times table. But what about other values? Can you modify the loop to make it do the 7 times table, for example? It should look like this:

```
for j in range(1, 13):
    print "%d x 7 = %d" % (j,j*7)
```

To alter the table, we have to change the 12 to a 7 twice. If we want another value, we have to change it again. Wouldn't it be better if we could enter the multiplier that we want? We can do so by replacing the values in the print string with another variable. Then we can set that variable before we run the loop:

```
multiplier = 12

for j in range(1, 13):
    print "%d x %d = %d" % (j, multiplier, j*multiplier)
```

That's our old friend the 12 times table. In fact, we already saw this technique—in Chapter 7 where we used a long string to generate the table. Now, to print the 7 times table , we need to change only the value of `multiplier`. Note that we have combined sequencing and loops. We have first a single command, `multiplier = 12`, followed *in sequence* by a `for` loop.

Looping the Loop

Let's take the previous example one stage further. Suppose we want to print out all of the multiplication tables from 2 to 12 (1 is too trivial to bother printing). All we really need to do is set the multiplier variable as part of a loop, like this:

```
for multiplier in range(2, 13):
    for j in range(1, 13):
        print "%d x %d = %d" % (j, multiplier, j*multiplier)
```

Notice that the part indented inside the first `for` loop is exactly the same loop with which we began. This example works as follows:

- We set `multiplier` to the first value (2), then go around the second loop as before.

- We set `multiplier` to the next value (3), and go around the inner loop again, and so on.

This technique is known as *nesting* loops. One snag is that all of the tables are merged together. We could fix that problem by printing out a separator line at the end of the first loop, like this:

```
for multiplier in range(2, 13):
    for j in range(1, 13):
        print "%d x %d = %d" % (j, multiplier, j*multiplier)
    print "------------------ "        # part of outer loop
```

Things to Ponder

Why are so many looping constructs available? Why not just have while *loops, given that all the others can be simulated with them?*

Can you think of any other loop constructs that you might want to use?

Can you use a loop to traverse a list from the back to the front (that is, starting at the highest index)?
(Hint: Look at the Python documentation for the range() *function.)*

Note that the second print statement lines up with the second for, so it is seen as the second statement in the outer loop sequence. Remember, the indention level is vitally important in Python. Experiment with using the separator to indicate which table follows, providing in effect a caption. (*Hint:* You will probably need to use the multiplier variable and a format string.)

Other Loops

Some languages provide more looping constructs. Nearly all languages, however, provide some kind of for and while loops. Other types of loops you might see are described here:

do-while
This loop works in the same way as a while loop, but the test appears at the end. Hence the loop body always executes at least once.

repeat-until
This loop is a variation on the do-while loop, but the logic of the test expression is reversed.

GOTO, JUMP, LOOP
Mainly seen in older languages, these loops (and others like them) usually set a marker in the code and then explicitly jump directly to it. They represent an unconditional transfer of control and so must be combined with a conditional or branching structure as described in Chapter 9.

Points to Remember

A for *loop repeats a block of code for a fixed number of iterations.*

A while *loop repeats a block of code until some terminating condition is met. The body of the loop may never execute if the terminating condition is initially false.*

Although other types of loops exist, for *and* while *are provided in virtually every programming language.*

Python's for *loops are really* foreach *loops—they operate on a list of items.*

Loops may be nested one inside another.

Python uses indentation to identify blocks of code.

Python uses a colon at the end of the control statement to indicate the start of the affected code block.

Chapter

9

Decisions, Decisions

What will we cover?

- *Selecting a path of execution for our program*

- *Simple either/or-type choices*

- *Multiple option choices*

The third of our fundamental building blocks is the *branching* or *conditional* construct. Such statements enable our program to execute one of several possible sequences of code depending on some condition.

In the early days of assembler programs, the simplest branch was a JUMP instruction, in which the program literally jumped to a specified memory address, usually if the result of the previous instruction was zero. Amazingly complex programs were written with virtually no other form of condition possible. When high-level languages came along, a new version of the JUMP instruction appeared—GOTO. This instruction performed an unconditional transfer of control to some other point in the program, usually defined in terms of a line number or special label.

Python doesn't provide a GOTO. You can see what it looked like in the following bit of code, which is written in an early dialect of BASIC:[1]

```
10 J = 5
20 IF J < 10 GOTO 40
30 Print "This line is not printed"
40 STOP
```

Even in such a short program, it takes a few moments to figure out what's going to happen, because you must search for line 40, which is the target of the GOTO. There is no structure to the code, so you have to figure it out as you read it. In large programs, it becomes virtually impossible, even for the programmer who originally wrote the code, to work out what's happening. For that reason, most modern programming languages either don't provide a direct JUMP or GOTO statement or the language authors discourage you from using it, perhaps by restricting its use to specific situations such as exiting a loop.

The most intuitively obvious conditional statement is the *if, then, else* construct. It follows the logic of English: if some Boolean condition is true, *then* a block of statements is executed; otherwise (or *else*), a different block is executed. The *else* part is optional.

Python does it this way:

```
if 12 > 10:
    print '12 is greater than 10'
```

You can also use an *else* condition:

```
import sys  # only to let us exit
j = 5
if j > 10:
    print "This is never printed"
else:
    sys.exit()
```

---

1. *You can actually run this code under QBASIC, which ships with Windows but is not installed by default. Find it on the Windows CD-ROM by using the* Files|Find *option and looking for* QBASIC.EXE.

Of course, any test condition can follow the `if`, so long as it evaluates to true or false (that is, a Boolean value). Also, as with loops, the indented section can be as long and complex as we want. It's not restricted to a single line, but it must be indented consistently.

Another point to note about *if, then, else* constructs is that you can reverse the logic of the test condition and swap the two conditional blocks, but the end result is the same. Thus the following code is functionally identical to the previous example:

```
import sys

j = 5

if j <= 10:  # reverse the logic, now "less than or equal"
    sys.exit()

else:
    print "This is never printed"
```

Chaining IF Statements

You can chain `if`/`else` statements together by nesting them one inside the other, as in the following example:

```
color = 'green'
score = 20
if color == 'red':  # see Note
    bonus = 0
else:
    if color == 'blue':
        bonus = score * 2
    else:
        if color == 'green':
            bonus = score / 2
        else:
            print "Found an unrecognized color"
print 'color: %s, score: %d, bonus: %d' % (color,score,bonus)
```

■ *Note:* We used == to test for equality in each if statement, whereas we used = to assign values to the variables. Using = when you mean to use == is one of the most common mistakes in programming Python. Fortunately, Python can identify this as a syntax error, but you might need to look closely to spot the problem.

One snag with this technique is that each test condition causes the indentation to increase. Thus, if you have a lot of tests, you need a wide screen to read the code.

Python provides an alternative *if/else* format for repeated tests:

```
if color == 'red':
    bonus = 0
elif color == 'blue':
    bonus = score * 2
elif color == 'green':
    bonus = score / 2
else:
    print "Found an unrecognized color"
```

Note the use of elif (short for "else if") and the fact that the indentation (all-important in Python) does not change with each test. It's also worth pointing out that both Python versions of this program are equally valid, but the second one is a little easier to read if many tests are involved.

One caveat applies with this type of test: you must get the order exactly right if you use anything other than equality for the test condition. Consider the following example:

```
value = 100
if value > 10:
    print 'This is OK'
elif value > 50:
    print 'Whoops, this is never seen'
else
    print 'nor is this'
```

Because the first test succeeded, the subsequent tests were never executed. We should have put the largest value test first.

Case Statements

Deeply nesting `if/else if/else` statements is such a common technique that many languages provide a special type of construct for it, often referred to as a *Case* or *Switch* statement (those are the keywords used in some languages). Python doesn't provide a case construct, so we will look at how another language, VBScript, handles this issue instead:

```
Select Case color{
    Case red:
        bonus = 0;
    Case blue:
        bonus = score * 2;
    Case green:
        bonus = score / 2;
    Case Else:
        WScript.Echo("Found an unrecognized color");
End Select
```

VBScript uses the keywords `Select Case` to test a variable—in this case, `color`—for a number of specific cases (values) and perform a corresponding action. We conclude with a default action if none of the tested values matches.

Combining Tests Using Boolean Expressions

With a series of nested `if` statements that have a common action as a result, we can combine the tests using Boolean operators. For instance, imagine that we have the following situation:

```
x = 15
if x < 10:
    print 'x is out of range'
elif x > 20:
    print 'x is out of range'
else:
    # do something with x
```

We can combine the first two tests using a Boolean OR operator:

```
if (x < 10) or (x > 20):
    print 'x is out of range'
else:
    # do something with x
```

A Gotcha with Combined Tests

Many programming languages, including Python, use a technique called *short-circuit evaluation* when dealing with Boolean expressions. That is, in the preceding example, if x were less than 10, the translator would never test whether it was greater than 20 because it knows that, regardless of the outcome, it will still have to print the error message.

Mostly this action is "a good thing" because it improves performance. It does mean, however, that if the second test contains a piece of code that does something essential, that piece of code might never be executed, leading to a very obscure bug in your program. The moral is that you should never write code that relies on all of your test conditions being evaluated.

Things to Ponder

Experiment with the Boolean operators described in Chapter 6. Can you create a simulation of the logic required to operate a stairway light—that is, one where either the top-of-stair switch or the bottom-of-stair switch will toggle the lamp on and off?

Can you use a combination of loops and conditionals to generate all of the prime numbers less than 50? Recall that a prime number is divisible only by itself and 1.
(Hint: You might find the modulo (%) operator useful here.)

Points to Remember

The else *part of an* if/else *statement is optional.*

The if/elif... *construct provides a more convenient way of writing long lists of* if/else if/... *expressions.*

Do not rely on the expressions within a test being evaluated. If the translator recognizes that the test is not necessary, it may not perform it.

Combine tests using Boolean operators if the associated actions are the same.

JUMP *and* GOTO *instructions seem easy to understand when you are writing code, but they are usually much more perplexing when you try to read it back later!*

Chapter

10

Conversing with the User

What will we cover?

- *How to prompt the user to enter data and how to read that data once entered*

- *How to read both numerical and string-based data*

- *How to read data input as command-line arguments*

So far our programs have dealt with only static data—data that, if need be, we can examine first and then write a program to match. Most programs aren't like that. That is, they get their data either from a user or from a data file. In this chapter, we'll look at ways to communicate with the user. In Chapter 12, we'll tackle reading and writing to files.

Obtaining Data from a User

Type in the following example and see what happens.

```
>>> print raw_input("Type something: ")
Type something: hjbbnmb
hjbbnmb
```

As you saw, `raw_input()` simply displays the given prompt and waits for the user to type in something. It captures whatever the user types in response and `print` then displays that response. We could, instead, assign the input to a variable:

```
>>> name = raw_input("What's your name? ")
What's your name? Alan
>>> print "Hi, %s, nice to meet you" % name
Hi, Alan, nice to meet you
```

The `raw_input` function has a cousin called `input`. Whereas `raw_input` collects the characters typed by the user and presents them as a string, `input` collects the characters and tries to form them into a number. For example, if the user types "1", "2", "3", then `input` will read those three characters and convert them into the number `123`.

Let's use `input` to decide which multiplication table to print:

```
multiplier = input("Which multiplier value do you want? ")
for j in range(1, 13):
    print "%d x %d = %d" % (j, multiplier, j * multiplier)
```

Command-Line Values

Another type of input comes from the command line. For example, imagine that you run your text editor as follows:

```
C:> notepad Foo.txt
```

How does Notepad read the file name?

In most languages, the system provides an array or list of strings containing the command-line words. Thus the first element will typically contain the command itself, the second element will be the first *argument*, and so on. Some languages might provide some kind of "magic variable" that holds the number of elements in the list.

In Python the argument list is held within the sys module and called argv (for "argument values"). You can determine the number of elements in sys.argv by using len(sys.argv). We can extract the elements using indexing or by iterating over the list. For example,

```
import sys
for item in sys.argv:
    print item

# recall that argv[0] is the program name so...

if len(sys.argv) > 1:
    print "the first real argument was:", sys.argv[1]
```

Note the use of an if statement to ensure that we don't try to print a nonexistent item. Checking for error scenarios is an important aspect of good programming that we'll discuss in Chapter 14.

Things to Ponder

Sometimes it's useful to read more than a single value at a time. Can you think of a way to do that with raw_input?

What happens if a user doesn't type a number when asked by input ()? *For example, what happens if he or she inputs "four" instead of "4"?*

That's about as far as we'll go with user input in this book. The approach outlined here is still very primitive, but you can still write useful programs with it. In the early days of UNIX or PCs, it was the only kind of interaction possible. Python can be used to write sophisticated GUI programs with windows, dialogs, and other user interaction elements, as we'll see later in the book. In particular, the case studies provide examples of getting input via a GUI in Python, although we won't explain much about how this technique works. Several tutorials are available for GUI programming that, with a good grounding in the essentials of programming, you should be able to follow without difficulty. Several of the resources listed in Appendix C include GUI tutorials.

Points to Remember

Use input *for reading numbers and* raw_input *for reading characters and strings.*

Both input *and* raw_input *can display a string to prompt the user.*

Command-line parameters can be obtained from the argv *list imported from the* sys *module in Python, where the first item is the name of the program file.*

Chapter

11

Modular Programming

What will we cover?

- *Different kinds of modules*

- *Using functions and modules*

- *Creating new functions and modules*

What's a Module?

The fourth element of programming is *modular programming*. In fact, using modules is not strictly necessary; using only sequences, loops, and branches, you can write some pretty impressive programs. As the programs grow larger, however, it becomes increasingly more difficult to keep track of what's happening and where. We really need a means to wall off some of the details so that we can concentrate on the problems at hand rather than the minutiae of how the computer works. Python already handles some of these tasks for us with its built-in capabilities. That is, it saves us from having to deal directly with the hardware of the computer—for example, how to read the individual keys on the keyboard.

Modular programming allows us to extend the built-in capabilities of the programming language. It packages up bits of program into modules that we can then "plug in" to our programs. The first form of module was the *subroutine*, which was a block of code to which you could jump (rather like the GOTO mentioned in Chapter 9); when the block completed, it jumped back to the location from which it was called. That specific style of modularity is known as a *procedure* or *function*. In Python and some other languages, the word *module* has taken on a specific meaning pertaining to the packaging of reusable code. We will look at that usage shortly, but first let's take a closer look at functions.

Using Functions

Before considering how to create our own functions, let's investigate how we can use the many, many functions that come bundled with any programming language (often referred to as the language's library). We've already encountered some of these functions in earlier chapters. Now let's see what these have in common and how we can use them in our programs.

The basic structure of a function call is as follows:

```
aValue = someFunction(anArgument, another, etc....)
```

Some variable takes on a value obtained by calling a function. The function can accept zero or many *arguments*, all of which it treats like internal variables. Functions can also call other functions internally. Let's consider some examples in Python to see how functions work.

```
>>> c = " "
>>> s = "a short string"
>>> import string
>>> words = string.split(s,c)
```

This function splits the string s into words using the character c as a separator (the default is whitespace[1]).

```
import string
times = "MORNING:EVENING:AFTERNOON"
periods = string.split(times,":")
print "Good—", periods[1]
```

---

1. *Whitespace is any character that is not a letter, number, punctuation mark, and so on—that is, the character appears white when printed. The most common examples are tabs and spaces.*

This code prints out "Good—EVENING".

val = pow(x,y)
Returns x^y.

```
x = 2    #  we'll use 2 as our base number
for y in range(0,11):
    print pow(x,y)    # raise 2 to power y
```

Here we generate values of y ranging from 0 to 10 and call the built-in pow() function,[2] passing two arguments, x and y. On each call, the current values of x and y are substituted into the call and the result is printed.

dir(m)
Another useful function built into Python is `dir`. When passed the name of a module, this function gives back a list of valid names—often functions—in that module. Try it on the built-in functions:

```
print dir(__builtins__)[3]
```

To use `dir` on any of the other modules you will have to import the module first. Otherwise, Python won't recognize the name and `dir` will fail with a `NameError`.

Before doing much else we need to talk about Python modules in a bit more detail.

Using Modules

We have mentioned and even used modules since the start of Section 2, but so far we haven't looked at them in any depth. Modules are important in Python because they are the mechanism that Python uses to allow you to add new capabilities to the language. You gain access to these new capabilities by importing modules. We'll see how to create modules shortly. For now, let's play with some of the standard modules that ship with Python.

---

2. *The exponentiation operator (`**`) is equivalent to the pow() function. Thus pow(2,4) yields the same result as 2**4.*
3. *Many special names exist in Python, most of which are marked by this double-underscore naming style.*

The sys Module

We met sys previously when we used it to exit from Python. It includes a whole bunch of other useful functions, too. To gain access to them, we must first import sys:

```
import sys  # make functions available
sys.exit()  # prefix with "sys"
```

If we plan to use a module's functions frequently, and we know that they won't have the same names as functions we have already imported from other modules or created in the importing module, then we can use the following code:

```
from sys import *  # import all names in sys
exit() # can now use without specifying prefix "sys"
```

Other Modules

You can import and use any of Python's modules in the same way, including modules that you create yourself. Let's take a quick tour of some of Python's standard modules and see what they have to offer (Table 11-1).

Table 11-1 Python Modules	Module Name	Description	See Chapter
	sys	Allows interaction with the Python system: exit—exit argv—access command-line arguments path—access the Python system path ps1—change the >>> Python prompt!	3, 10
	os	Allows interaction with the operating system: rename—rename file or directory system—execute an operating system-level command mkdir—create a directory getcwd—find the current working directory	12
	string	Allows manipulation of strings: atoi/f/l —convert string to integer/floating point/long find—find substring split—break into "words" upper/lower—case conversion	12, 22, 23

Table 11-1	Module Name	Description	See Chapter
Python Modules (continued)	math	Allows access to many mathematical functions: sin, cos, and so on—trigonometrical functions log, log10—natural and decimal logarithms ceil, floor—ceiling and floor pi, e—natural constants	7
	time	Time (and date) functions: time—get the current time (expressed in seconds from some date that is operating system-dependent) gmtime—convert time in secs to UTC (GMT) localtime—convert to local time mktime—inverse of localtime sleep—pause program for n seconds	11

These modules are merely the tip of the iceberg. Literally dozens of modules are provided with Python, and you can download just as many more. Look at the documentation to find out how to do Internet programming (sockets, cgi), graphics (Tkinter), build databases (dbm), and more.

The important point is that most programming languages have these basic functions either built-in or as part of their standard libraries. Always check the documentation before writing a function—it may already exist!

Defining New Functions

Now that we know how to use the existing functions and modules, how can we create new functions? Simply by *defining* them. That is, we write a statement that tells the interpreter that the following block of code should be treated as a function.

Let's create a function called times that can print out a multiplication table for any value that we provide as an argument. In Python, the times() function looks like this:

```
def times(n):
    for i in range(1,13):
        print "%d x %d = %d" % (i, n, i*n)
```

It is called in this way:

```
print "Here is the 7 times table..."
times(7)
```

Notice that we use the keyword def to create the function definition. As usual, the body is indented under the def statement, which in turn is terminated with a colon. We define a *parameter* called n and pass an *argument* of 7. The local variable n inside the function takes the value 7 when we call it. We can define as many parameters as necessary in the function definition, and the calling programs must provide corresponding values for each parameter.

Note that this function does not return any value. Some languages reserve the term *function* for cases where values are returned and use the more specific term *procedure* for cases where no value is returned. In Python we describe both types of construct as a function. We can, in fact, have our functions return a value if necessary, as we'll see next.

Returning Values from Functions

What if we wanted to define a function that calculates a required value? We use the keyword return. In Python, the code has the following form:

```
def isPositive(v):⁴
    if v >= 0:
        return 1     # 1 is true
    else:
        return 0     # 0 is false
```

We can us it like this:

```
x = input('Enter a number')
if isPositive(x):
    print x, 'is positive'
```

Here the isPositive function returns a Boolean value that we can use in a conditional statement.

If you need to return multiple values, then you have several options. In most languages, you can pass a list to the function as an argument and have the function modify the contents of the list. The code can then read the values out of the list (see the "Changing Parameter Values" sidebar for more details).

---

4. *This function could be implemented more concisely by simply returning* (v >= 0) *as a Boolean result. I have used the more explicit version above to make it as clear as possible how the function works.*

Python offers another mechanism, which is to return a list or a tuple. A tuple can contain many values and we can assign multiple variables to the contents of a tuple. For example:

```
>>> a,b,c = (1,2,3)
>>> print a,b,c
1 2 3
```

Thus we can define a function that returns a list of all factors of a number and we can call that function as follows:

```
>>> def factors(aNumber):
...        factorList = []    # create an empty list
...        for i in range(2, aNumber/2+1):
...             if (aNumber % i) == 0:
...                  factorList.append(i)
...        return ( factorList )
...
>>> print 'The factors of 48 are:', factors(48)
The factors of 48 are: [2, 3, 4, 6, 8, 12, 16, 24]
```

A built-in function that does a similar thing is divmod. It returns both the division value and the remainder in a tuple:

```
>>> print '3 into 10 gives %d remainder %d' % divmod(10,3)
3 into 10 gives 3 remainder 1
```

Passing Values to Functions

In the factor example, we passed a single argument to the function, which in turn was defined with a single parameter. We can have as many parameters as we like in a function definition. For example, the divmod function takes two arguments and returns two values in a tuple.

Defining a function to take multiple parameters is simple. We just list the names within the parentheses, like so:

```
def myFunction(aValue, anotherValue):
    # do something with aValue and anotherValue
    # simply consider them as local variables,
```

```
# although you should be careful about
# changing them (see sidebar)
```

If we define a function with two parameters then we must pass two arguments when we call it. One exception to this rule arises when the function uses *default parameters*. We'll look at them now.

Default Parameter Values

Some programming languages, including Python, allow you to define default values for a parameter—that is, if no value is provided, the function assumes a default value. One sensible use for default values would be in a function that returns the day of the week. If we call it with no value, we mean today; otherwise, we provide a day number as an argument. For example:

```
# a day value of -1 => today
def dayOfWeek(DayNum = -1):
    # days indices must correspond to the values returned by
    # the Python localtime tuple element, with Monday = 0
    days = ['Monday','Tuesday',
            'Wednesday','Thursday',
            'Friday', 'Saturday', 'Sunday']

    # check for the default value
    if DayNum == -1:
        # use the time module functions to get current time
        # see the sidebar and the official documentation
        import time
        theTime = time.localtime(time.time())
        DayNum = theTime[6]    # pick out today's value
    return days[DayNum]
```

We need to use the `time` module only if the default parameter value is involved, so we can defer the `import` operation until we need it. This approach would provide a slight performance improvement if we never had to use the default value feature of the function.

We can call this function as follows:

```
print "Today is: %s" % dayOfWeek()
# remember that in computer-speak we start from 0
# and the Python convention is that the first day is Monday
print "The third day is %s" % dayOfWeek(2)
```

Time Function Return Values

Python's time functions use several different representations of time. One is based on a numerical representation, another uses a tuple of values, and a third uses an ASCII string representing the tuple in a readable format.

`time()` returns a floating-point number giving the number of seconds since the *epoch*. The epoch is an arbitrary date and time that varies among operating systems. You can find the epoch on your system by evaluating `localtime(0)`.

`localtime(t)` returns a tuple with nine elements. The Python documentation describes the contents as follows:

year (for example, 1993)
month (1-12)
day (1-31)
hour (0-23)
minute (0-59)
second (0-59)
weekday (0-6, Monday is 0)
Julian day (1-366)
Daylight Savings flag (-1, 0, or 1)

`ctime(t)` returns an ASCII string representing the time value, `t`, passed as a floating-point value.

```
>>> print time.ctime(0)
Thu Jan 01 00:00:00 1970
```

When using the `time` module, check the documentation to ensure that the value you get back is in the format required. If it isn't, use one of the conversion functions, as we did in the `dayOfWeek` example.

When you mix nondefault and default parameters in a function definition, the default parameters must go last. When the function is called, all of the non-default values must be provided along with as many as necessary of the default ones. The rest of the parameters will assume the default values.

One minor "gotcha" applies to default parameters. When Python reads a function definition with a default value, it creates a single copy of the default value, which is then used by every call to that function. If the default is a list, the function could potentially modify that list. Subsequent calls to the function would then use the modified default value. This result may not be what the caller expects. It's probably best not to modify the value of default parameters within the function, but rather to operate on a copy[5].

Changing Parameter Values

You might think that one way to return a value to the calling code would be by changing the value of the argument passed in. This approach will not work in most cases, however.

Consider this example:

```
>>> def incr(n):
...     n = n+1
...
>>> i = 2
>>> incr(i)     # this does not change i
>>> print i
2
```

Now let's try another example:

```
>>> def parrot(L):
...     L.append('squawk')
...
>>> P = []
>>> parrot(P)    # adds "squawk" to the list!
>>> print P
['squawk']
```

---

5. *An easy way to copy a list in Python is to use list slicing; for example,* L2= L1[:] *creates a new list,* L2, *with the same contents as* L1.

This time we succeeded in modifying the list. Why? We changed the *content* of the list but not the list itself. If within `parrot` we had tried to assign a new list to `L`, it wouldn't have worked. This technique can be used to return multiple values from a function. Because it can also be a source of bugs, be careful how you use it.

Objects are special types of containers—they contain properties and methods. Thus, if an object is passed to a function and the function changes its properties, then the original object will be changed in the same way as a list. The technical term for this behavior is passing parameters *by value.* That is, the parameter takes on the value of, or becomes a copy of, the argument. Where the argument is a container or object, then the value is the value of the *reference* to the container.

Python allows you to pass arguments only by value, but some other languages permit you to pass the arguments by *reference.* In that case, you can change the parameter value inside the function and the change will be reflected back to the caller.

Word Counting

Another useful function that returns a value might be one that counts the words in a string. You could use it to calculate the number of words in a file by adding the totals for each line together.

The code for this function might look something like the following (it won't work, so don't bother trying it):

```
def numwords(s):
    list = split(s)      # list with each element being a word
    return len(list)     # return number of elements in list


for line in file:
    # accumulate totals for each line
    total = total + numwords(line)
print "File had %d words" % total
```

This example uses a common design technique whereby you sketch out how you think the code should look but don't bother to use absolutely correct code. This technique is sometimes known as *pseudocode* or, in a slightly more formal style, *Program Description Language* (PDL). The advantage of pseudocode is that it allows us to concentrate on the concepts needed to solve the problem rather than the details of the language syntax. Once we understand how to solve the problem, we can translate the pseudocode into our target language fairly easily. In this case, it also allows us to gloss over the fact that we don't know how to handle files yet.

Once we've had a closer look at file and string handling a little later in the book, we'll return to this example and do it properly.

Creating Our Own Modules

Now we are able to create our own functions and call them from other parts of our program. That's good because it can save us a lot of typing and, more importantly, makes our programs easier to understand—we can forget about some of the details after we create the function that hides them. (This principle of wrapping up the complex bits of a program inside functions is called *information hiding*, for obvious reasons.) How can we use these functions in other programs? We can create a module.

A Python module is nothing special. It's just a plain text file full of Python statements. In most cases, these statements are function definitions. For example, when we type

```
from sys import *
```

we ask Python to copy the contents of the sys module into our program, almost like a cut-and-paste operation.[6]

To recap, we create a module by creating a Python file containing the functions we want to reuse in other programs. Then we import our module in exactly the same way as we import the standard modules. That sounds easy enough, so let's try it.

Important Note

If you didn't start Python from the same directory in which you stored the `timestab.py` file, then Python might not be able to find the file and might report an error. If so, then you can create an environment variable called `PYTHONPATH` that holds a list of valid directories to search for modules (in addition to the standard modules supplied with Python). Creating environment variables is a platform-specific operation that I assume you either know how to do or can find out!

---

6. *It's not really what happens but as a concept it's close enough. In some programming languages (notably C++), the translator does really copy module files into the current program, although a module file in C++ is very different from a Python module.*

Type the function below into a new text file and save the file in the current directory or a directory that you have added to your PYTHONPATH environment variable (see the "Important Note" sidebar) with the name timestab.py:

```
def print_table(multiplier):
    print "--- Printing the %d times table ---" % multiplier
    for n in range(1,13):
        print "%d x %d = %d" % (n, multiplier, n*multiplier)
```

Now at the Python prompt type:

```
>>> import timestab
>>> timestab.print_table(12)
```

Hey, presto! You've created a module and used it.

Next, let's look at files and text handling and then, as promised, revisit the business of counting words in a file.

Things to Ponder

When you create a function, you have a choice of putting it either in your main program file or in a separate module file and importing it. When would it be best to put the function in a separate module?

| Points to Remember |

Use modules by importing them.

Use functions by calling them, passing arguments within parentheses, and assigning the results to variables as appropriate.

Define functions using def *and use* return *to pass back results.*

Define modules by putting code into text files with a .py *suffix. Most of the code should be in the form of function definitions.*

The PYTHONPATH *environment variable tells Python where to look for module files.*

Chapter
12

Handling Files and Text

What will we cover?

- *Opening a file*

- *Reading and writing to text files*

- *Dealing with very long files*

- *Counting words in a file*

Handling files often poses problems for beginning programmers, although the reason for this uncertainty puzzles me slightly. Files in a programming sense are no different from files that you use in a word processor or other application: you open them, do some work, and then close them again.

The major difference is that when programming, you access the file sequentially[1]—that is, you read one line at a time, starting at the beginning and working through to the end. In practice, the word processor often does the same, holding the entire file in memory while you work on it and then writing it all back out when you close the file. Another difference between the two kinds of files is that you normally open the file as read-only or write-only when programming, whereas a word processor appears to read and write the same file. When writing files, you have the option of creating a new file from scratch, overwriting an existing one, or appending to an existing one.

---

1. *It's possible to create random access files for faster access, but this approach imposes some restrictions and is fairly unusual in practice. In this book we'll stick with simple sequential access.*

Input and Output Files

Let's assume that a file exists called `menu.txt` and that it holds a list of meals:

```
Menu for Tue Aug 08 08:28:04 2000


spam & eggs
spam & chips
spam & spam
```

Now we will write a program to read the file and display the output—like the cat command in UNIX or the `type` command in DOS.

```
# open the file to read(r)
inp = open("menu.txt","r")# see Note 1


# read the complete file into a list, then print each item
for line in inp.readlines():# see Note 2
    print line


# close it again
inp.close()
```

∎ *Note 1:* The open() function takes two arguments. The first is the file name (which may be passed as a variable or a literal string, as we did here). The second is the *mode*. The mode determines whether we are opening the file for reading (r) or writing (w), and whether the file is for ASCII text (the default) or binary usage (see the "Handling Binary Files" sidebar).

∎ *Note 2:* We read and close the file using a function name preceded by the file variable. This notation is known as *method invocation*. As you may recall from Chapter 6, it means that the file variable is an object. A file object therefore contains methods that operate on files,[2] and we automatically gain access to these methods every time we create a file object by using open().

Handling Large Files

In the preceding example, we read the entire file into memory. Now consider how you might cope with large files that require more memory than is available. First, you would need to read the file one line at a time (by using `readline()` instead of `readlines()`). Then, you might use a `line_count`

---

2. *The functions operate specifically on the file to which our variable refers.*

variable that is incremented for each line and then tested to see whether it is equal to 25 (for a 25-line screen). If so, you would request that the user press a key (Enter, for example) before resetting line_count to zero and continuing. You might like to try that case as an exercise...

Really, that's all there is to it. You open the file, read it in, and manipulate it as desired. When you're finished, you close the file.

Handling Binary Files

Binary files are not arranged in lines with a recognized *end of line* marker. Thus, when working with binary files, we need to treat them slightly differently than text files. First, we must specify in the open function that we want to work with binary data by passing an extra "b" in the mode argument:

```
>>> b_out = open('bin.dat','wb')
```

To write binary data, we must first *pack* the data using the struct module. See the struct documentation in the Python Library Reference for all of the operations possible. For our example, we will write four integers to the file bin.dat:

```
>>> b_out.write(struct.pack('4i',1,2,3,4))
>>> b_out.close()          # close file to force write
```

When reading a binary file, we must specify how much data we want to read. We use an optional length argument to the read() method:

```
>>> b = open('bin.dat','rb')
>>> bytes = b.read(4)
```

Before we can print the bytes, we must convert them into a printable format. The ord() function will handle that task for us:

```
>>> for c in bytes: print ord(c)
...
1
2
3
4
```

We have read back the first four bytes from bin.dat, the same file we created earlier. It's not usually necessary to handle binary files, but Python can help you when it is required.

To create a COPY command in Python, we simply open a second file in write mode and write the lines to that file instead of printing them. For example:

```
# create the equivalent of: COPY MENU.TXT MENU.BAK
# open the files to read(r) and write(w)
inp = open("C:\\MyFiles\\menu.txt","r")
outp = open("menu.bak","w")


# read file line by line until eof (line becomes false)
# copy each line to output file
line = inp.readline()
while line:
    outp.write(line)
    line = inp.readline()
print "1 file copied..."


# close the files
inp.close()
outp.close()
```

We processed the file line by line this time, so we don't need to worry about file size limits. Once we reach the end of the file, line will be empty, which counts as false in the test condition. A print statement appears after the loop to reassure the user that something actually happened. This kind of user feedback is usually a good idea.

Backslash Characters in Strings

Did you notice that we used \\ in the file name in the last program? That's because Python uses the "\" character to indicate that the next character is special. To put a real \ into the string, we must use two of them—that is, \\ means \. These special combinations are known as escape sequences. Some other combinations include the following:

```
\n      newline
\t      tab
\nnn    the character represented by nnn, where nnn is an octal (base 8)
        number (for example, \033 is the escape character)
```

You can find other examples in the Python Reference Documentation.

In Python, the forward slash character can be used as a separator in file paths in both UNIX and Windows. This usage eliminates the need to use an escape character but may feel unnatural to some Windows/DOS users.

Modifying an Existing File

If you need to modify an existing file, you have two choices. First, you can either read the existing file into memory (assuming you have enough room); close the input file; process the data; reopen the same file, this time using write mode; and write the data back out, overwriting the original contents. Alternatively, you can create a new output file; write the results to it; and use the os module to remove the original file and rename the new file to the original file name. The second method is more complicated but is the only choice if the file might be too large to fit in memory. It is also safer—if the computer or program crashes during the operation of the program, the first method could result in the loss of the original file whereas the second method guarantees that the data will remain safe.

For example, imagine that we want to create a program that will write a new header line to the top of our menu file each day. We could use the following code:

```
import os, time
try:#try/except is explained in chapter 14
    # initialize files and variables
    menu= open('menu.txt','r')
    outf = open('menu.tmp','w')
    header = 'Menu for %s' % time.ctime(time.time())

    # write header and append menu body
    outf.write(header + '\n')
    lines = menu.readlines()
    for i in range(2,len(lines)):
        outf.write(lines[i])
    outf.close()
    menu.close()

    # manipulate files
    os.rename('menu.txt','menu.bak')
    os.rename('menu.tmp','menu.txt')
    os.remove('menu.bak')
except:
    print 'ERROR: Failed to create new menu'
```

Appending to Files

One final twist is that you might want to append data to the end of an existing file. One way to accomplish that goal would be to open the file for input, read the data into a list, append the data to the list, and then write the entire list out to a new version of the old file. If the file is short, this approach does not present any problems; if the file is very large, perhaps exceeding 100MB, then you will probably run out of memory. Fortunately, we can pass another mode ("a") to open( ) that allows us to append directly to an existing file just by writing. Even better, if the file doesn't exist, this mode will open a new file just as if you'd specified "w".

As an example, let's assume we have a log file that we use for capturing error messages. We don't want to delete the existing messages, so we choose to append the error:

```
def logError(msg):
  err = open("Errors.log","a")
  err.write(msg)
  err.close()
```

In the real world, we would probably want to limit the size of the file in some way. A common technique is to create a file name based on the current date. When the date changes, we automatically create a new file. This approach helps maintainers of the system find the errors for a particular day and archive old error files if they are not needed.

Counting Words

Let's revisit that word counting program mentioned in Chapter 11. Recall the pseudocode we crafted earlier:

```
def numwords(s):
    list = split(s) # list with each element being a word
    return len(list) # return number of elements in list
for line in file:
    # accumulate totals for each line
    total = total + numwords(line)
print "File had %d words" % total
```

We now know how to get the lines from the file, so let's think about the body of the numwords() function. First, we want to create a list of words in a line. In the Python reference documentation for the string module, we find a function called split() that breaks a string into a list of fields separated by whitespace (or any other character we define). Finally, after again referring to the documentation, we see that the built-in function len() returns the number of elements in a list, which in our case should be the number of words in the string—exactly what we want.

Putting all of that together, the final word count program has the following form:

```
import string
def numwords(s):
    # need to qualify split() with string module
    list = string.split(s)
    return len(list)   # return number of elements in list


inp = open("menu.txt","r")
total = 0   # initialize to zero; also create variable


for line in inp.readlines():
    # accumulate totals for each line
    total = total + numwords(line)
print "File had %d words" % total


inp.close()
```

Things to Ponder

Are there other ways of copying files in Python, using the facilities of the operating system?
(Hint: Look up the Python Library Reference.)

What kinds of errors might occur when processing files?

The program is not perfect because it counts the "&" character as a word (although maybe you think it should...). Also, it can be used only on a single file (menu.txt). We can, however, convert it to read the file name from the command line (argv[1]) or using the raw_input() function, as we saw in Chapter 10. I leave that challenge as an exercise for you.

Points to Remember

After opening a file, you must read it before you can work on the data.

If reading a file line by line, remember to check for the end of the file.

Chapter

13

A Touch of Style

What will we cover?

- *Some more about comments*

- *An alternative type of comment*

- *How variable names can be comments too*

Style in programming, as in so many other aspects of life, is a very personal thing. It is essentially subjective, and what one programmer believes is good style will be seen by another as gross. Some consensus has arisen in a few areas, however. I'll try to stick to those areas of agreement, but in the process I will inevitably introduce a few of my own opinions. I apologize in advance.

More Comments

Describing Lines of Code

We introduced comments in Chapter 5, but we'll take a more detailed look at them here. Although commenting code is one of the most important programming aids, beginners often feel that it's just wasted effort on first acquaintance. Comments are lines in the program that describe what's going on. They have no effect on how the program operates, but are purely decorative. That doesn't mean they are useless, however. They have an important role to play—they tell the programmer what's going on and, more importantly, *why.*

Comments in code are especially important if the programmer reading the code isn't the one who wrote it or if a long time has passed since the code was written. Once you've been programming for a while, you'll really appreciate good comments. From this point forward, we will comment the code fragments we write. Gradually, the amount of explanatory text will diminish as the explanation appears in comments instead.

To recap, Python uses a # symbol as its comment marker. Anything following a # is ignored.

```
v = 12      # give v the value 12
x = v*v     # x is v squared
```

This code shows very bad commenting style. Your comment should not merely state what the code does—we can see that for ourselves! It should explain *why* the code takes this approach. Consider this code fragment from a (fictitious) larger program:

```
sph = 3600    # 3600 is num of secs in an hour
s = t * sph   # t is elapsed time in hours, so convert to secs
```

These comments are much more helpful because they explain the significance of the "magic number" 3600. Of course, it would be even more helpful if we had named t something more descriptive, such as elapsed_time.

Describing Paragraphs

It's quite common in a long program to split the code into groups of logically connected statements. A number of comment lines will then precede each group to summarize the purpose of that code. That use is illustrated in the following fictitious block of code (it doesn't do anything, so don't bother trying it):

```
# Having opened the file we can write out the
# assembled blodgit details
saveToFile(blodgit1, outputFile)
saveToFile(blodgit2, outputFile)
processBadBlodgits(badList, outputFile)
```

Note that comments are just like any other statement in the program, except that they don't execute. The block of code above is a sequence of five statements, two of which are comments and three of which are executable lines of code.

Comments as a Debugging Tool

So far we've considered what comments can add to your code. Because comments are ignored by the translator, they can also be used as a convenient mechanism for making part of your program invisible. This technique can help isolate those parts of a program that are causing a problem. For example, you might replace a function call with a hard-coded assignment, as in this snippet of code:

```
# f = foo()
f = 12     # temp: debugging only
if f > 10:
    print 'f = , f
```

We commented out the call to `foo()`, replacing it with a simple assignment that we know will pass the conditional test. This approach can help us decide whether the commented-out statements are the source of our problems. Of course, you need to remember to restore the code to its proper state once the problem has been located and fixed.

Describing Files

It is also common practice to put a block of comments at the top of a file. This block should provide information such as the author of the file; the date when the program was written; the current version number; a list of the services, constants, and objects provided by the file; and usually a history of changes. It might also include some general advice on how the features of the file should be used, outlining prerequisites and environment variables that are assumed to exist, for example. Normally, this book omits these comments to save space. In production programs, however, it's a good idea to include them.

The following example is the header I created for one of the case study files in Chapter 22:

```
#############################
# Module: grammar
# Created: A.J. Gauld, 1999, 8, 19
#
# Function:
# Counts paragraphs, lines, sentences, "clauses," chargroups
```

```
# words, and punctuation for a prose-like text file. It assumes
# that sentences end with [.!?] and paragraphs have a blank
# line between them. A "clause" is simply a segment of a
# sentence separated by punctuation (it's brain-dead but maybe
# someday we'll do better!).
#
# Usage:
# Basic usage takes a file name parameter and outputs all
# stats. It's expected that a second module will use the
# functions provided to produce more useful commands.
##############################
```

In most other programming languages you would also provide function headers. Python offers a better technique, as we'll see next.

Documentation Strings

Python includes a feature that is rarely found in other programming languages but is very useful, particularly when working from the interactive prompt. We mentioned documentation strings in passing when discussing triple-quoted strings in Chapter 6, but now we will look at how they are used.

The basic concept is very simple: Python considers a string placed immediately after a function definition statement to be documentation for that function and stores it in the special variable __doc__ as an attribute of the function object. As a consequence, we can view this documentation by printing the __doc__ attribute. Here is an example:

```
>>> def foo():
        """ Foo is a test function of no use to anyone!
    Foo is just being used to try out doc strings."""
        return 7
>>> foo()
7
>>> print foo.__doc__
Foo is a test function of no use to anyone!
    Foo is just being used to try out doc strings.
```

Documentation strings have not been used much in the examples in this book to save space; the text usually explains the workings of the functions. Of course, the strings don't have to be triple-quoted—any string will do. Triple-quoted strings allow the documentation to spill over several lines, which is usually necessary for worthwhile documentation. A helpful convention is to give a very brief (typically one-line) summary of the function, then miss a line before providing full documentation. Many of the built-in functions and standard modules include documentation strings. Try printing a few out to see what they look like.

Variable Names

The variable names we have used so far have been fairly meaningless, mainly because they have simply illustrated techniques. In general, your variable names should reflect what you want them to represent. For example, in our 12 times (multiplication) table exercise, we used `multiplier` as the variable to indicate which table we were printing. That name is much more meaningful than simply `m`, which would have worked just as well and required less typing.

Variable names involve a trade-off between comprehension and effort. Generally the best choice comprises short but meaningful names. An excessively long name becomes confusing and is difficult to get right consistently. For example, we could have used `the_table_that_we_are_printing` instead of `multiplier` as the variable name, but the former is far too long and not really much clearer.

Another convention exists as to how to write multiple-word names. In days of yore, programmers tended to separate words with underscores. Today, the trend is to make the first word start with a lowercase letter and have subsequent words begin with uppercase initial letters. The preceding example would thus become `theTableThatWeArePrinting`. It still isn't a good name, but it does illustrate the technique.

Other naming conventions include making class names start with an uppercase letter and making constant variables be all uppercase. Note that these conventions are merely guidelines. The programming language does not enforce them or expect you to follow these rules. Nonetheless, they do bring a bit of consistency, which ultimately makes the code easier to understand.

Things to Ponder

Why is consistency useful in writing programs?

Comments have many uses. We have touched on a few here, but can you think of others?

Do you use a naming convention in any of your other activities? Filing documents, perhaps?

Some extremely exotic naming conventions have been devised involving cryptic sequences of letters either prefixing or postfixing the real variable name. These sequences usually represent the type of the data that the variable holds or that the function returns. This style of naming convention is often referred to as Hungarian notation. It offers little real benefit and can, if not scrupulously maintained, become a source of error in its own right. Some find it useful, however. As ever, try it and use it if it helps you.

Points to Remember

Comments can describe more than just individual lines of code.

Comments can make your code invisible, which is useful in debugging.

Documentation strings provide a kind of online help facility.

Meaningful variable names make a program easier to read and understand.

Chapter

14

Handling Errors

What will we cover?

- *The various types of errors*

- *Two ways to detect expected errors*

- *Ways to cope with unexpected errors*

- *Ways to generate errors for other people to handle*

To this point, we've assumed that everything we do in our programs will work. In the real world, that's just not the case—files don't always exist, we sometimes run out of memory, and users don't always enter the expected data. As programmers, we need to handle all of these eventualities (and more) in our programs. Some errors, such as a nonexistent file, can be anticipated; others may be unexpected. Anticipated errors can be handled in either of two ways: the traditional way or the modern (exceptional) way. Unexpected errors were once nearly impossible to handle, but modern languages provide a way of detecting virtually any error, even the unexpected ones.

The Traditional Way of Error Handling

Traditionally when programmers do something, such as using a function, the result of the function can be tested for validity. For example, if you try to index past the end of a list you will get an error. Two strategies have commonly been employed to deal with these kinds of situations:

1. Include the error code in the result of the function.

2. Set a global variable to an error status.

In either case, the programmer is responsible for checking whether an error has occurred and taking the appropriate action. In Python, this might look something like the following imaginary code:

```
import somemodule
if not somemodule.oldfunction():    # check that it worked OK
    handleErrors()
else:
    # continue with rest of program
```

This strategy can result in production-quality programs where almost half of the code is devoted to testing every action for success. The resulting code is cumbersome and hard to read (but in practice, the majority of programs in use today work in this way). A consistent approach is essential if silly mistakes are to be avoided.

The Exceptional Way of Error Handling

In more recent programming environments, such as Python, an alternative way of dealing with errors has developed. Known as *exception handling*, it works by having functions `raise` or `throw` an *exception*. The system then forces a jump out of the current block of code to the nearest exception-handling block. The programming environment provides a default handler that catches all exceptions, typically prints an error message, and then exits. We've seen this kind of default error handler in action so far in our Python programs.[1]

---

1. When Python reports an error, it generates a stack trace. This concept originates from the idea that the flow of control in a program starts with some function called at the top level, perhaps at the Python prompt. This main function, in turn, calls other functions, which call others, and so forth. These functions can be envisioned as being stacked one on top of the other (in practice, that's usually how the translator implements it, using a stack data structure). Python's error handler prints out the current position in each function within the stack as a debugging aid.

The exception-handling block is coded much like an `if`/`else` block:

```
try:
    # program logic goes here
except ExceptionType:
    # exception processing for named exception goes here
except AnotherType:
    # processing for a different exception goes here
except:
    # this section catches any error not caught above
else:
    # here we tidy up if NO exceptions were raised
```

Another type of exception block allows us to tidy up after an error. Called a `try...finally` block, it is typically used for closing files, flushing buffers[2] to disk, and more. The `finally` block is *always* executed regardless of what happens in the `try` section.

```
try:
    # normal program logic
finally:
    # here we tidy up regardless of the
    # success/failure of the try block
```

One snag with this construct is that you can't combine it with an except block except by nesting `try` statements:[3]

```
try:
    try:
        # try to do whatever it is
    except:
        # handle any exceptions
finally:
    # close files etc.
```

---

2. When writing to a file the computer saves the information in RAM until a certain minimum quantity is stored in a bit of memory called a "buffer." We can force the system to write out the contents of the buffer before it's full by issuing a `flush` command. One reason you shouldn't just switch off a PC is that the buffers may not get flushed and you could lose data!

3. This restriction leads to the question of which **try** construct should be on the inside of the nesting. My preference is to put the `try`/`finally` outermost; other programmers favor placing it inside. Use the tactic with which you feel most comfortable. Most of all, try to be consistent.

Generating Errors

What happens when we want to generate exceptions to be caught elsewhere, such as from a module? In that case, we use the `raise` keyword in Python. In the following example, we will create a module that raises an error and then show how we could import that module and catch the error:

```
# module raiserr.py
def div42():
    denominator = input("What value will I divide 42 by? ")
    if denominator == 0:
        raise "zero denominator" # raise a string error
    else:
        return 42/denominator
```

This code raises a "string object" exception of value "zero denominator," which can be caught by a `try/except` block. Now we can import the module and test it from the Python interactive prompt:

```
>>> from raiserr import *
>>> print div42()
what do you want to divide 42 by? 7
6
```

The normal case works as expected, but what about the exception?

```
>>> print div42()
what do you want to divide 42 by? 0
Traceback (innermost last):
  File "<pyshell#80>", line 1, in ?
    print div42()
  File "<pyshell#78>", line 4, in div42
    raise "zero denominator"
zero denominator
```

Finally, let's see this code in use from a script file, where we use `try`/`except` to catch the error:

```
# module testerr.py
import raiserr
try:
    div42()
except "zero denominator":
    print "number must be non zero"
```

The raiserr module raises a "string object" exception of value "zero denominator," which can be caught by the `try`/`except` block in testerr.py.

Nesting Error Handlers

What happens if errors occur in a block of code that is nested within an error-handling block? Or what if we define a `try` block inside another `try` block? Where will the error be handled? The easiest way to find out is to try it! The first situation looks like the following code:

```
try:
    print 'Starting a try block'
    for i in [1,2,3]:
        print i/0 # divide by zero!
    print 'Ending a try block'
except:          # catches any error
    print 'Caught an error'
    i = 0        # faulty attempt to fix error
    print i/0    # divide-by-zero error raises new exception
```

Here we jump straight out of the `for` block to the error handler. Because we don't jump to the outer block, the `print 'Ending....'` statement never executes. The error inside the except section is not caught, however, and it results in a Python error trace from the default handler. Thus we should create a `try`/`except` construct at the very topmost level of our programs to be sure to catch *any* unhandled exceptions anywhere in our programs; we should restrict the error handling within that except block to things that are unlikely to cause problems, such as printing fixed-string error reports. This tactic is a very useful way of ensuring that our users never face the rather severe error reports and code tracebacks generated by Python itself.

The second question dealt with what happens with nested `try` blocks:

```
try:
    print 'First try'
    try:
        print 'Second try'
        print 'fred' ** 3 # will raise a TypeError
    except TypeError:
        print 'Caught a TypeError'
except TypeError:
    print 'Shouldn't see this'
except:
    print 'Caught something unexpected'
```

The innermost except catches the error and prevents it from reaching either the specific or generic handlers at the top level. If we want to propagate the error to the top level, we would add a `raise` statement to the innermost handler:

```
# code as above
    except TypeError:
        print 'Caught TypeError'
        raise# propagates current exception up one level
except TypeError:
    print 'This time we handle it here, too'
# continue as before
```

Log Files

One final error-handling feature that you may want to consider, especially for server-based programs or programs requiring little or no user interaction, is the logging of error information. Log files can contain much more detail than would be presented in an error message to a user and should be aimed at assisting support personnel (which might be you!) to figure out retrospectively what went wrong. You probably want to capture the following kind of information:

- Date and time

- Function being executed (maybe a full or partial "stack trace,"[4] if possible)

- The type of error

- If it's a multiuser environment, the user ID

---

4. *A stack trace lists the functions executed, all the way back to the top level. Python generates one by default. It is not something you would normally want the user to see, but a stack trace is very useful to the programmer in working out what went wrong.*

Things to Ponder

How many "expected error" situations can you think of? Consider errors you have experienced in the applications you use regularly. What kinds of error dialogs do you see?

One advantage of the try/except *style of error handling is that the application code is easier to read because it contains fewer spurious* if/else *constructs. What disadvantages can you see in the* try/except *style of error handling? What happens if you want to return to the main body of code after handling the error?*

Another important issue to be addressed when using log files is disk space. If you continue writing out error information to a single file, the log file will eventually get very large, perhaps even filling the disk. The result will make you very unpopular! If you decide to implement an error-logging facility, make sure you also provide a means to archive old error logs or to overwrite the old file every day. It is often a good idea to make logging a switchable option, perhaps by setting an environment variable or similar trick, so that logging is used only when errors start occurring.

Points to Remember

All programs will encounter errors. Try to anticipate them and either handle errors internally or notify the user in the friendliest way possible.

If you can anticipate an error, then deal with it as close to the point of occurrence as possible. You may then be able to continue without disturbing the user.

Unanticipated errors should be caught and a user-friendly error message presented.

It can be helpful to log detailed information about errors in a file. This log file aids in debugging later, and the user can e-mail the file to you if necessary. Be careful to provide some mechanism to limit the size of the file via archiving, overwriting, or another technique.

Section

3 Advanced Topics

This section is quite different from the previous sections in that it is a potpourri of topics. You can read each topic as a separate, independent entity, or you can simply carry on reading through the book in sequence. It's up to you. Don't let the title "advanced topics" put you off—the topics are more advanced than what we've covered so far, but they don't involve rocket science.

Chapter
15

Recursion

What will we cover?

- *Defining recursion*

- *Showing how it can be applied*

Recursion is a genuinely advanced topic and for most applications you don't need to know anything about it. Occasionally, it is so useful that it is invaluable, so I present it here for your study. Don't panic if it doesn't make sense immediately. Just leave it for now and return to it later when you have a bit more confidence and experience in programming.

What Is Recursion?

Despite the earlier statement indicating that looping is one of the cornerstones of programming, it is, in fact, possible to create programs without an explicit loop construct. Some languages, such as Lisp, don't have a loop construct like `for` or `while`; instead, they use a technique known as *recursion*. Recursion is a very powerful technique for some types of problems, so we'll look at it now.

Recursion simply means applying a function as a part of the definition of that same function. Thus the definition of GNU (the source of much free software) is said to be recursive because GNU stands for "GNU's Not UNIX." That is, GNU is part of the definition of GNU! The key to making this idea work is that **a terminating condition must exist,** such that the function branches to a non-recursive solution at some point. (The GNU definition fails this test and so gets stuck in an infinite loop.)

Let's look at a simple example. The mathematical factorial function is defined as being the product of all the numbers up to and including the argument; the factorial of both 0 and 1 is 1. Thinking about this function, we see that another way to express this concept is by stating that the factorial of N is equal to N times the factorial of (N – 1).

```
0! = 1
1! = 1 x 1 = 0! x 1 = 1
2! = 1 x 2 = 1! x 2 = 2
3! = 1 x 2 x 3 = 2! x 3 = 6
N! = 1 x 2 x 3 x .... (N-2) x (N-1) x N = (N-1)! x N
```

We can express the factorial function in Python as follows:

```python
def factorial(n):
    if (n < 0):
        raise 'negative number error'
    elif (n == 0) or (n == 1):
        return 1
    else:
        return n * factorial(n-1)
```

First, we check that no negative numbers are passed as arguments, because the factorial of a negative number is undefined. Next, we return 1 if either 0 or 1 is passed as an argument. Finally, we return the product of the argument n and the result of calling `factorial` with n–1 as the argument. Because we decrement n each time and test for n equal to 1, the function must eventually complete.

Try out this program by putting the code in a module and then typing at the Python prompt:

```
>>> from factorial import factorial
>>> factorial(5)
125
>>> factorial(-2)
Traceback (innermost last):
    File "<stdin>", line 1, in ?
    File "factorial.py", line 3, in factorial
      raise 'negative number error'
negative number error
```

Notice how `factorial(-2)` generated a traceback containing our exception string. If we were using `factorial` in a real program, we could have caught that error by using a `try/except` handler and either generated a user-friendly error message or converted the number to a positive value and called `factorial()` with it as an argument.

Writing the factorial function without recursion involves quite a bit more code. You need to loop over a list of all numbers from 1 to N, multiplying the current total by the current item. Try writing this program as an exercise, and compare your result to the function above.

Recursing over Lists

The other area where recursion is very useful is in processing lists. If we can

- test for an empty list and
- generate a list minus its first element

then we can easily use recursion to process lists.

Consider the trivial case of printing each element of a list of strings using a function called `printList()`:

```
def printList(L):
    if L:
        print L[0]
        # for [1:] - see "slicing" in the
        # Python Reference Manual
        printList(L[1:])
```

If L is true—nonempty—we print the first element and then process the rest of the list. Because we always remove the first element before recursing, we will eventually pass printList an empty list and the process will terminate.

For a simple list containing single values, this program is a trivial exercise involving a normal for loop. Consider, however, what happens if the list is complex and contains other lists within it. We must test whether the first item is a list and, if so, call printList() recursively. If it's not a list, then we simply print it. Having dealt with the first item, we continue to process the rest of the list. Let's write this program. Create a new module called printlist.py containing the following function:

```
def printList(L):
    # if it's empty, do nothing
    if not L: return
    # if it's the same type as a list, call
    # printList on first element
    if type(L[0]) == type([]):
        printList(L[0])
    else: # not a list so just print the element
        print L[0]
    # process the rest of L
    printList(L[1:])
```

At the Python prompt, try this:

```
>>> aList = ['a',['b','c',['d','e']],'f',[],'g']
>>> from printlist import printlist
>>> printList(aList)
a
b
c
d
e
f
g
```

If you try to write printList() using a conventional loop construct, you'll find your task much more difficult. Recursion makes a very complex task comparatively simple.

Things to Ponder

Can you think of other uses for recursion? How about spell checking a document that has other documents embedded within it?

There is a catch (of course!). Recursion on large data structures tends to eat up memory. Thus, if you are short of memory or plan to process very large data structures, the more complex conventional code may be safer.

Points to Remember

Recursion can replace loops in many cases.

Recursion requires a terminating condition to prevent infinite loops.

Recursion can be a heavy drain on memory.

Chapter 16 Namespaces

What will we cover?

- *The what and why of namespaces*

- *The implementation of namespaces in Python*

A Little History Lesson

"What's a namespace?," you ask. Actually, this concept is surprisingly difficult to explain. The difficulty arises not because namespaces are especially complicated, but because every language defines them differently. The concept is relatively straightforward: a *namespace* is a space or region, within a program, where a name (such as a variable, or class) is valid. Sometimes the term *scope* is used instead of namespace.

Namespaces evolved because early programming languages (like BASIC) had only *global variables*—that is, variables that could be seen throughout the whole program, including inside functions. This characteristic made maintenance of large programs difficult, because it was easy for one bit of a program to modify a variable without other parts of the program realizing it—this spillover was called a *side-effect*. To get around this problem, later languages (including modern BASIC versions) introduced the concept of namespaces.[1]

To illustrate the concept, think about a large office block. Everyone in a single office refers to each other by first name. When a conversation starts involving people from different offices, the names may be qualified as "Joe from Accounting" or "Sally in Marketing." This qualification makes it clear which Joe or Sally is meant. Accounting and marketing are namespaces within that organization.

Python's Approach

In Python, every module creates its own namespace. To access those names, we must either precede them with the name of the module or explicitly import the names we want to use into our module's namespace. Nothing new there—we've been doing the same thing with the `sys` and `string` modules. In a sense, a class definition also creates its own namespace. Thus, to access a method or property of a class, we need to use the name of the instance variable (or the class name[2]) first.

Python permits only three namespaces:

1. Local—names defined within a class, function, or method

2. Module—names defined within a file

3. Built-in—names defined within Python itself that are always available

Figure 16-1 illustrates how these namespaces fit together. In the figure, variables defined within any particular box can be accessed only from within their own box or from within boxes contained within their own box. Thus functions within the module cannot directly access variables declared in other functions or those declared within classes, but they can access variables defined at the module level.

So far, so good. But what happens when variables in different namespaces have the same name? Or when we need to reference a name not in the current namespace?

---

1. C++ has taken this idea to extremes by allowing programmers to create their own namespaces anywhere within a program. This flexibility is useful for library creators who might want to keep their function names unique when their libraries are mixed with libraries provided by another supplier.
2. It's possible to call a method of a class by using the class name and passing the object as the first argument. In addition, some methods or attributes are shared between class instances and are also accessed by using the class name. More on this idea in Chapter 17.

Figure 16-1
Hierarchy of
namespaces

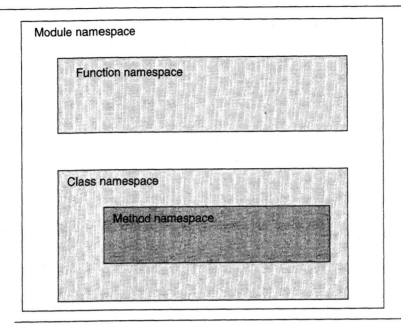

Avoiding Name Clashes in Functions

Let's consider the first situation. If a function refers to a variable called **X** and an **X** exists within that function (local namespace), then that **X** variable is the one that will be seen and used by Python. If you want to assign a value to a variable outside the local namespace (which would normally create a new local variable), you must declare the external variable to be **global**. It's the programmer's job to avoid name clashes such that a local variable and a module variable of the same name are not both required in the same function—in such a case, the local variable will mask the module one.

We can see this idea demonstrated in the following code snippet:

```
>>> modValue1 = 7
>>> modValue2 = 9
>>> def lumberjack():
...     global modValue1 # use the external one
...     modValue1 = 42
...     modValue2 = -7 # local since no global statement
...
```

```
>>> lumberjack()
>>> print modValue1, modValue2
42 9
```

Notice that modValue1 was modified by lumberjack( ), but modvalue2 wasn't changed because no global[3] statement appeared inside the function.

In general, you should minimize your use of global statements. It's usually better to pass the variable in as an argument and then return the modified variable.

Name Resolution

The second situation, in which a name that does not exist within the current local namespace is referenced, is resolved as follows. The function will look first within its local namespace; if it can't find the name there, it will then look at the module namespace; if the name is not there, it will turn to the built-in namespace.

We can see this idea at work in the following example (which merely illustrates the point and has no practical use):

```
# variables within the module namespace
W = 5
Y = 3


# parameters are like function variables
# so X is in the local namespace
def spam(X):
    # tell function to look at module level and
    # not create its own W
    global W
    Z = X*2 # new variable Z created in local namespace
    W = X+5 # use module W as instructed above

    if Z > W:
        # print function comes from built-in namespace
```

---

3. *The term global is a throwback to the days when a variable defined at the module level was actually visible to any other module in a program; indeed, it was globally visible. This strategy is generally a bad idea because it becomes difficult to keep track of when and where changes to a variable occur. The closest match that Python provides is a module-level variable that must be prefixed by the module name to be used in any other module. Somehow the **global** tag has persisted. Python uses it to mean a variable outside the currently local namespace.*

```
            print "2 x X is greater than X + 5"
            return Z
    else: return Y # no local Y, so uses module version
```

When we import a module such as sys, we make the name sys available locally. We can then access names within the sys module namespace by qualifying the name as we've seen previously. The statement:

```
from sys import exit
```

brings the exit function into the local namespace. We cannot use any other sys names—not even sys itself.

We can use a wildcard character to import all of the internal names into our modul. You should do so only if you are sure that it won't conflict with your local names. Use the following format:

```
from petshop import *
```

If you need to access only one or a few names, you can import those names explicitly:

```
from petshop import parrot, goldfish
```

Things to Ponder

Why is overusing global *considered a bad practice?*

One surprising consequence of this statement is that we cannot access *any* other members of the petshop module—not even the name petshop itself. We have access to only parrot and goldfish.

Points to Remember

Python has three namespaces: local, module, and built-in.

If you want to refer to a variable outside a function, declare it as global.

To gain access to a module's namespace, use import.

Namespaces are handled very differently by different languages. When learning a new language, be sure to check the namespace (or scoping) rules.

Chapter

17

Object-Oriented Programming

What will we cover?

- *A definition of classes and objects*
- *Polymorphism and how to use it*
- *Reusing code by inheritance*

What Is Object-Oriented Programming?

In this chapter, we examine what might have been termed an advanced topic until about five years ago. Today, object-oriented programming is the norm. Languages like Java and Python embody the concept so much that you can do very little without coming across objects somewhere. So what's it all about?

Some of the best introductions to this topic appear in the following books:

- *Object Oriented Analysis* by Peter Coad and Ed Yourdon
- *Object Oriented Design with Applications* by Grady Booch (the first edition, if you can find it)

- *Object Oriented Software Construction* by Bertrand Meyer (you definitely want the second edition)

These references increase in depth, size, and academic exactitude as you go down the list. For most nonprofessional programmers' purposes, the Coad and Yourdon is sufficient and very easy to read. For a more programming-focused introduction, try *Object Oriented Programming* by Timothy Budd (second edition). Budd covers the key features of object-oriented programming using several different languages to demonstrate the techniques. Finally, for a whole heap of information on all topics object-oriented, try the following Web site:

```
http://www.cetus-links.org
```

Assuming that you have neither the time nor the inclination to research these books and links right now, this chapter provides a brief overview of the most important concepts. (*Note:* Some people find object-oriented programming difficult to grasp; others "get it" right away. Don't worry if you come under the former category—you can still use objects even without really "seeing the light".)

Data and Function—Together

Objects are collections of data and the functions that operate on that data. These components are bound together so that you can pass an object from one part of your program to another and the receiver automatically gets access to not only the data *attributes* but also the available *operations*. For example, a string object would store the character string and also provide methods to operate on that string—search, change case, calculate length, and so on.

Objects use a *message passing* metaphor, whereby one object passes a message to another object and the receiving object responds by executing one of its operations, known as a *method*. Thus a method is invoked on receipt of the corresponding message by the owning object. Various notations are used to represent this relationship. Python uses a dot. Thus, for a fictitious `Widget` class:

```
w = Widget()     # create new instance, w, of Widget
w.paint()        # send the message "paint" to it
```

This code would invoke the `paint` method of the `Widget` object, `w`.

Defining Classes

Just as data has various types, so objects can have different types. A collection of objects with identical characteristics is known as a *class*. We can define classes and create instances of them, which are the actual objects. We can then store references to these objects in variables in our programs.

Let's look at a concrete example to clarify this idea. We will create a Message class that contains a string—the message text—and a method to print the message.

```
class Message:
    def __init__(self, aString):
        self.text = aString
    def printIt(self):
        print self.text
```

■ *Note 1:* One method of this class called __init__ , is a special method known as a *constructor*. A constructor is called automatically by Python when a new object instance is created (that is, constructed). Any variables assigned (and hence created in Python) inside this method will be unique to the new instance.[1] Python includes a number of special methods like this one, nearly all of which are distinguished by the __xxx__ naming format.

■ *Note 2:* Both the methods defined in the code have a first parameter of self. This name is a convention that indicates the object instance. As we will see, the interpreter fills in this parameter at runtime, rather than the programmer supplying it. Thus printIt is called with no arguments: m.printIt(). During the execution of the printIt method, self will take on the value m.

■ *Note 3:* We named the class Message, with a capital "M." This capitalization is purely a convention but a popular one, not just in Python but in other object-oriented languages. A related convention says that attribute and method names should begin with lowercase letters and subsequent words in the name should begin with uppercase letters. Thus a method called "calculate current balance" would be written calculateCurrentBalance.

You may want to briefly revisit Chapter 6 and look again at user-defined types. The Python address example should be a little clearer now. Essentially the only type of user-defined type in Python is a class.

---

1. *It's possible to create variables that are shared by all instances, known as class variables. We won't say much about class variables in this book, but you can read about them in the Python Language Reference and Tutorial.*

Using Classes

Having defined a class, we can now create instances of our `Message` class and manipulate them:

```
m1 = Message("Hello world")
m2 = Message("So long, it was short but sweet")


note = [m1, m2]    # put the objects in a list
for msg in note:
    msg.printIt()    # print each message in turn
```

In essence, you treat the class as if it were a standard Python data type, which was, after all, the purpose of the exercise! Notice that any arguments passed to the class constructor "function" are passed in turn to the class's `__init__()` method by Python.

Same Thing, Different Thing

So far, we know how to define our own classes, create instances of these classes, and assign the instances to variables. We can then pass messages to these objects that trigger the methods we have defined. There's also another element to this object-oriented stuff, and in many ways it's the most important aspect of all.

If we have two objects of different classes, each supporting the same set of messages[2] but with its own corresponding methods, then we can collect these objects together and treat them identically in our program, but the objects will behave differently. This ability to behave differently in response to the same input messages is known as *polymorphism*.

For example, we might use polymorphism to get a number of different graphic objects to draw themselves on receipt of a "paint" message. A circle is a very different shape from a triangle, but provided both have a paint method, we, as programmers, can ignore the difference and just think of them as "shapes."

---

2. *Classes with identical message sets are said to support the same* interface. *Some programming languages, like Java, treat interfaces as a key part of their object-oriented strategy. Python is much more informal about this aspect of object-orientation.*

Let's look at an example where we calculate the areas of two shapes. First, we create `Square` and `Circle` classes:

```
class Square:
    def __init__(self, side):
        self.side = side
    def calculateArea(self):
        return self.side**2


class Circle:
    def __init__(self, radius):
        self.radius = radius
    def calculateArea(self):
        import math
        return math.pi*(self.radius**2)
```

Note that we obtained the value of pi from the `math` module. It is common to find standard constants defined in such modules.

Now we can create a list of shapes (either circles or squares) and then print out their areas:

```
list = [Circle(5), Circle(7), Square(9),
        Circle(3), Square(12)]


for shape in list:
    print "The area is: ", shape.calculateArea()
```

If we combine these ideas with modules, we get a very powerful mechanism for reusing code: Put the class definitions in a module—say, `shapes.py`—and then simply import that module when we want to manipulate shapes. This approach is exactly what has been taken with many of the standard Python modules, which is one reason why the process of accessing methods of an object closely resembles the process of using functions in a module.

Inheritance

Inheritance is often used as a mechanism to implement polymorphism. Indeed, in many object-oriented languages it is the only way to implement polymorphism. It works as follows: A class can inherit both attributes and operations from a *parent class* or *superclass*.[3] Thus a new class that is identical to another class in most respects does not need to reimplement all of the methods of the existing class. Instead, it can *inherit* those capabilities and then *override* those that it wants to handle differently (like the `calculate Area` method in our earlier example).

Once again, an example might illustrate this idea best. We will use a class hierarchy of bank accounts where we can deposit cash, obtain our balances, and make a withdrawal. Some of the accounts provide interest (which, for our purposes, we'll assume is calculated on every deposit—an interesting innovation in the banking world!), and others charge fees for withdrawals.

The `BankAccount` Class

First, let's consider the attributes and operations of a bank account at the most general (or abstract) level. It's usually best to first consider the operations and then provide attributes to support these operations. For a bank account, we can perform the following operations:

- Deposit cash

- Withdraw cash

- Find the current balance

- Transfer funds to another account

To support these operations, we will need a bank account number (for the transfer operation) and the current balance. We'll assume the account name is the account number; if we were accessing real accounts, as in a database, we would need to have an explicit account number of some sort. Also, to simplify the example, we'll use a single floating point number to store the balance and other monetary values.[4]

---

3. You may also see the term base class used. These terms ... standardization has occurred yet.
4. This choice of data type is a bad idea in real financial applications, floating point numbers have limited accuracy and integers are a better choice for storing financial amounts. Doing so requires converting all input and output amounts to/from a decimal representation to a single number. While not difficult, this task would simply complicate our example ...

We can create the following class:

```
#create an exception string for later use - Note 1,2
BalanceError = "Sorry you have only $%9.2f in your account"


class BankAccount:
    def __init__(self, initialAmount):
        self.balance = initialAmount
        print "Account created. Balance = %9.2f" % self.balance

    def deposit(self, amount):
        self.balance = self.balance + amount

    def withdraw(self, amount):
        if self.balance >= amount:          # Note 3
            self.balance = self.balance - amount
        else:
            raise BalanceError % self.balance

    def getBalance(self):
        return self.balance

    def transfer(self, amount, account):
        try: # Note 4
            self.withdraw(amount)           # Note 5
            account.deposit(amount)
        except BalanceError:
            print BalanceError
```

■ *Note 1:* There is no standard error type `BalanceError`, so we need to create one ourselves. It's simply a string variable!

■ *Note 2:* We used a `%9.2f` specifier in the `BalanceError` format string. It simply tells Python to format the output using nine characters with two digits after the decimal point.

■ *Note 3:* We check the balance before withdrawing money and raise an error if insufficient funds are available.

■ *Note 4:* We use exceptions to handle errors in the `transfer` method—specifically, to catch our own `BalanceError` exception.

■ *Note 5:* The `transfer` method uses the `BankAccount`'s `withdraw/deposit` *member functions* or methods to do the transfer. This tactic is very common in object-oriented programming and is known as *self-messaging*. It means that derived classes can implement their own versions of `withdraw/deposit` but the `transfer` method can remain the same for all account types.

The *InterestAccount* Class

Next, we use inheritance to provide an account that adds interest (we'll assume 3%) on every deposit. It will be identical to the standard `BankAccount` class except for the `deposit` method. So we simply override that method:

```
class InterestAccount(BankAccount):
    def deposit(self, amount):
        BankAccount.deposit(self,amount)
        self.balance = self.balance * 1.03
```

And that's it. We begin to see the power of object-oriented programming. All of the other methods have been inherited from `BankAccount` (by putting `BankAccount` inside the parentheses after the new class name). Notice also that `deposit` called the superclass's `deposit` method rather than copying the code. If we modify `BankAccount`'s `deposit` method to include some kind of error checking, the subclass will gain those changes automatically.

The *ChargingAccount* Class

This account is identical to a standard `BankAccount` class except that it charges $3 for every withdrawal. As with the `InterestAccount` class, we can create a class that inherits from `BankAccount` and modifies the withdraw method.

```
class ChargingAccount(BankAccount):
    def __init__(self, initialAmount):
        BankAccount.__init__(self, initialAmount)
        self.fee = 3     # Note 1

    def withdraw(self, amount):
        BankAccount.withdraw(self, amount+self.fee)     # Note 2
```

■ *Note 1:* We store the fee as an instance variable so that we can change it later if necessary. Notice that we can call the inherited __init__ just like any other method.

■ *Note 2:* We add the fee to the requested withdrawal and call BankAccount's withdraw method to do the real work. We introduce a side effect here in that a charge is automatically levied on transfers as well, but that's probably what we want.

Testing Our System

To verify that our program works, try executing the following piece of code (either at the Python prompt or by creating a separate test file).

```
from bankaccount import *


# First a standard BankAccount
a = BankAccount(500)
b = BankAccount(200)
a.withdraw(100)
# a.withdraw(1000)
a.transfer(100,b)
print "A = ", a.getBalance()      # should be 300
print "B = ", b.getBalance()      # should be 300


# Now an InterestAccount
c = InterestAccount(1000)
c.deposit(100)
print "C = ", c.getBalance()      # should be 1133


# Then a ChargingAccount
d = ChargingAccount(300)
d.deposit(200)
print "D = ", d.getBalance()      # should be 500
d.withdraw(50)
print "D = ", d.getBalance()      # should be 447
d.transfer(100,a)
print "A = ", a.getBalance()      # should be 400
print "D = ", d.getBalance()      # should be 344
```

```
# Finally transfer from charging account to the interest one
# The charging one should charge and the interest one should
# add interest
print "C = ", c.getBalance()      # should still be 1133
print "D = ", d.getBalance()      # should still be 344
d.transfer(20,c)
print "C = ", c.getBalance()      # should now be 1187.59
print "D = ", d.getBalance()      # should now be 321
```

Things to Ponder

When designing a class, is it necessary, or even desirable, to model every aspect of the class? If building a Pen class, would you build it in the same way for a stock control application as you would for a graphics program?

Many object-oriented languages, including Python, allow you to inherit from more than one super-class, an ability known as multiple inheritance. Can you think of an situation where you might want to do that? Can you think of any disadvantages? What happens if several of the superclasses have methods with the same name?

Now uncomment the line a.withdraw(1000) to see the exception at work. That's all there is to it.

This example is quite straightforward but still shows how inheritance can be used to quickly extend a basic framework with powerful new features.

We've seen how we can build up the example in stages and how we can put together a test program to check if it works. Our tests were not complete in that we didn't cover every case and we could have included more checks, such as what to do if an account is created with a negative amount.

This chapter has given you a small taste of object-oriented programming. You're now ready to try some of the online tutorials or read one of the books mentioned at the beginning of this chapter to obtain more information and examples. We'll also use object-oriented programming in some other chapters and in the case studies.

Points to Remember

Objects encapsulate data and the functions that operate on that data.

Objects receive messages and respond by executing methods.

Different object types can respond to the same message by executing different methods, known as polymorphism.

Classes can inherit the attributes and operations of another class, then override those operations that they wish to handle differently. They can also add new operations. Also, classes create their own namespaces.

Methods can access bits of the current object (including other methods) by using the self *parameter.*

Chapter

18

Event-Driven Programming

What will we cover?

- *Building an event loop*

- *Building an application to handle events*

- *Introducing Tkinter, Python's GUI toolkit*

So far we have considered only batch-oriented programs. Recall that batch-oriented programs start, do something, and then stop. Event-driven programs start, wait for events, and stop only when told to do so—by an event. How do we create an event-driven program? We'll look at this issue in two ways: by simulating an event environment and by creating a very simple GUI program that uses the operating system and environment to generate events.

Simulating an Event Loop

Every event-driven program includes at least one loop that catches received events and processes them.[1] The events may be generated by the operating system, as happens with virtually all GUI programs, or the program itself may look for events, as is often the case in embedded control systems such as those used in cameras.

In this chapter, we will create a program that looks for precisely one type of event—keyboard input—and processes the results until some quit event is received. In our case, the quit event will be the space character. We will process the incoming events in a very simple manner, by printing the ASCII code for that key. The main program body starts the event loop and calls the event-handling functions when a valid event is detected. (The event handlers must be defined before the loop.)

```
# msvcrt works only on Windows
# the curses module for Linux offers
# a similar function: stdscr.getch()
import msvcrt, sys


# event handlers go here (see CD Rom)
# better tell the user what to do
print """
Type a key to see its ASCII value.
Hit the space bar to end
"""
# create the event loop
while 1:  # 1 is true, so loop forever
    key = msvcrt.getch()
    if key != ' ':
        # handle special keys; real code is second
        if (key == '\000') or (key == '\xe0'):
        key = msvcrt.getch()
        # dispatch normal events
        doKeyEvent(key)
    else:  # send the quit event
        doQuitEvent(key)
```

---

1. *Okay, I lied. Some event-driven programs don't have an event loop. Instead, they rely on hardware interrupts that are associated with blocks of code—usually functions or object methods. This type of programming is quite specialized however and for our purposes we will assume that event-driven programs include a hidden event loop.*

```
# define the event handlers - "the application"
def doKeyEvent(key):
    print ord(key)     # print the ASCII code


def doQuitEvent(key):
    sys.exit()
```

What we do with the events is of no interest to the main loop, as it simply collects the events and passes them to the event handlers. This independence of event capture and processing is a key feature of event-driven programming.

If we were creating this program as a framework for use in lots of projects, we would probably include a call to an initialization function at the start and a cleanup function at the end. The programmer could then use the loop part as is and provide his or her own initialization, processing, and cleanup functions.

In fact, that's exactly what most GUI-type environments do. The event loop is embedded in the operating environment or framework, and applications are contractually required to provide the event-handling functions and hook them into the event loop in some way.

Let's see an example of that approach in action as we explore Python's Tkinter GUI library.

A GUI Program

For this exercise, we'll use Python's Tkinter toolkit. This is a wrapper around the Tk toolkit that was originally written as an extension to Tcl and is also available for Perl. The Python version is an object-oriented framework that is considerably easier to work with than the original procedural Tk version. We will not dwell on the GUI aspects of this toolkit, but rather focus on the style of programming. Tkinter is used to handle the event loop and the programmer must then create the initial GUI and process the events as they arrive.

In the example, we create an application class KeysApp, which creates the GUI in the __init__ method and binds the space character to the doQuitEvent method. The class also defines the required doQuitEvent method. The GUI consists of a text entry widget, whose default behavior is to echo characters typed by the user.

Creating an application class is quite common in object-oriented event-driven environments, because much synergy exists between the concepts of events being sent to a program and messages being sent to an object. The two concepts map to each other very easily. An event-handling function thus becomes a method of the application class.

Having defined the class, we create an instance of it and then this instance calls the `mainloop` message, whose corresponding method is inherited from the Tkinter `Frame` widget. The code looks like this:

```
from Tkinter import *


# create the application class that defines the GUI
# and the event-handling methods
class KeysApp(Frame):
    def __init__(self):
        Frame.__init__(self)
        self.txtBox = Text(self)
        # we use '<space>' for the space character
        # otherwise Tkinter just sees an empty string
        self.txtBox.bind('<space>', self.doQuitEvent)
        self.txtBox.pack()
        self.pack()
    def doQuitEvent(self,event):
        import sys
        sys.exit()
# create an instance and start the event loop
myApp = KeysApp()
myApp.mainloop()
```

In the previous version of this program, we printed the ASCII codes of the keys rather than the alphanumeric versions of printable keys as we do here. There's nothing to prevent us from capturing all of the keypresses and doing the same thing. To do so, we would add the following line to the `__init__` method:

```
self.txtBox.bind("<Key>", self.doKeyEvent)
```

We would also add the following method to process the event:

```
def doKeyEvent(self,event):
    str = "%d\n" % event.keycode    # see Note 1
    self.txtBox.insert(END, str)
    return "break"                  # see Note 2
```

■ *Note 1:* The key value is stored in the `keycode` field of the event. I had to look at the source code of `Tkinter.py` to find that out—remember that curiosity is a key attribute of a programmer!

▌*Note 2:* `return "break"` is a magic signal to tell Tkinter not to invoke the default event processing for that widget. Without that line of code, the text box will display the ASCII code followed by the actual character typed, which is not what we want here.

Things to Ponder

Why is event-driven programming so popular for embedded systems like camera control? What other electronic devices have you seen that might use event-driven control systems?

Although it is usually possible to take a sequential batch-style program and convert it to an event-driven style, it is usually much more difficult to do the reverse and create a batch-oriented program from an event-driven one. Why?

One interesting feature of this program is that it works for the special keys on the keyboard such as the Shift and Alt keys. The previous version of the code ignored these keys. These differences reflect the underlying mechanisms used by Tkinter and `msvcrt.getch()` to access the keyboard.

That's enough for now. This example isn't meant to be a tutorial on Tkinter; however, several books on using Tk and Tkinter have been published. We will return to Tkinter in the case studies, where we will use it to illustrate one way of encapsulating batch mode programs in a GUI for improved usability and explore more of the Tkinter building blocks.

▌Points to Remember▐

Event-driven programs depend on an event loop, which is usually provided by the programming environment or operating system. You can write one yourself if necessary.

The functionality of event-driven programs resides in their event handler functions or methods.

Event handlers can make no assumptions about what has happened previously or what may happen later in the program. They must be wholly self-contained, or stateless.

Tkinter is a Python GUI toolkit that is suitable for small-scale GUI programs and is portable across many computing platforms.

Chapter
19

Regular Expressions

What will we cover?

- *What is a regular expression?*
- *How can we create them?*
- *How can we use them?*

Definition

Regular expressions are groups of characters that describe a larger group of characters. They describe a *pattern* of characters for which we can search in a body of text. Regular expressions are very similar to the concept of wildcards used in file naming on most operating systems, whereby an asterisk (*) can be used to represent any sequence of characters in a file name—for example, *.py means any file ending in .py. In fact, file name wildcards are a very small subset of regular expressions.

Regular expressions are extremely powerful tools, and most modern programming languages either include built-in support for their use or have libraries or modules available that you can use to search for and replace text based on regular expressions. A full description of this topic is beyond the scope of this book. At least one whole book is dedicated to regular expressions, however, and if your interest is piqued by this discussion you can turn to some of the references listed in Appendix C for more information.

One interesting feature of regular expressions is that they share similar structures with programs. Regular expressions are patterns constructed from four types of smaller units:

- Single characters
- Wildcard characters
- Character ranges or sets
- Groups that are surrounded by parentheses

Because groups are a unit, you can have groups of groups and so on, to an arbitrary level of complexity. We can combine these units in ways reminiscent of a programming language using sequences, repetitions, or conditional operators. We'll look at each of these options in turn. To try out the examples in this chapter, you will need to import the `re` module and use its methods. For convenience, I will assume you have already imported `re` in most of the examples shown here.

Sequences

As ever, the simplest construct is a sequence and the simplest regular expression is just a sequence of characters:

```
red
```

This sequence will match, or find, any occurrence of the three letters "r", "e", and "d" in order in a string. Thus the words *red*, lette*red*, and c*red*ible would all be picked up because they contain "red" within them. To provide greater control over the outcome of matches, we can supply special characters (known as *meta-characters*) to limit the scope of the search (Table 19-1).

Meta-characters	Location	Example
^red	Only at the start of a line	red ribbons are good
red$	Only at the end of a line	I love red
/Wred	Only at the start of a word	it's redirected by post
red/W	Only at the end of a word	you covered it already

Table 19-1
Meta-
characters used
in sequences

The meta-characters in Table 19-1 are known as *anchors* because they fix the position of the regular expression within a line or word. Several other anchors are defined in the **re** module documentation that are not covered in this chapter.

Sequences can also contain wildcard characters that can substitute for any character. The wildcard character is a period. Try this:

```
>>> import re
>>> re.match('be.t', 'best')
<re.MatchObject instance at 864460>
>>> re.match('be.t', 'bess')
```

The message in angle brackets tells us that the regular expression **be.t** passed as the first argument matches the string **best** passed as the second argument. The **be.t** will also match **beat**, **bent**, **belt**, and so on. The second example did not match because **bess** didn't end in **t**, so no MatchObject[1] was created. Try a few more examples to see how this matching works.

The next unit is a range or set. It consists of a collection of letters enclosed in square brackets. The regular expression will search for any *one* of the enclosed letters.

```
>>> re.match('s[pwl]am', 'spam')
<re.MatchObject instance at 7cab40>
```

---

1. *A MatchObject is a regular Python object with various helpful properties. One of these properties includes the location of the expression within the string, although for the* **match()** *function that will always be the beginning.*

By putting a "^" sign as the first element of the group, we can say that it should look for any character *except* those listed. Thus in the example

```
>>> re.match('[^f]ool', 'cool')
<re.MatchObject instance at 864890>
>>> re.match('[^f]ool','fool')
```

we can match `cool` and `pool` but we will *not* match `fool`.

Finally, we can group sequences of characters, or other units, together by enclosing them in parentheses. This ability is not particularly useful in isolation, but it is helpful when combined with the repetition and conditional features.

Repetition

We can create regular expressions that match repeated sequences of characters by using other special characters. We can look for a repetition of a single character or group of characters by using the meta-characters listed in Table 19-2.

	Character	Meaning	Example
Table 19-2 Meta-characters used in repetition	?	Means zero or one of the preceding character. The zero part can trip you up if you aren't careful.	`python1?y` matches: `pythony` `python1y`
	*	Looks for zero or more of the preceding character.	`python1*y` matches: `pythony` `python1y` `python11y` `python111y`
	+	Looks for one or more of the preceding character.	`python1+y` matches: `python1y` `python11y` `python111y`
	{n,m}	Looks for n to m repetitions of the preceding character.	`fo{1,2}` matches: `fo` or `foo`

All of the repetition characters listed in Table 19-2 can be applied to groups of characters, too. For example:

```
>>> re.match('(.an){1,2}s', 'cans')
<re.MatchObject instance at 862760>
```

The same pattern will also match: `cancans`, `pans`, or `canpans`, but not `bananas`.

One caveat applies with the `{m,n}` form of repetition: it does not limit the match to only n units. Thus the example in Table 19-2, `fo{1,2}`, will successfully match `fooo` because it matches the `foo` at the beginning of `fooo`. If you want to limit how many characters are matched, you must place an anchor or a negated range after the multiplying expression. In our case, `fo{1,2}[^o]` would prevent `fooo` from matching because it says match one or two "o"s followed by anything other than an "o".

Greedy Expressions

Regular expressions are said to be *greedy*. That is, the matching and searching functions will match as much as possible of the string rather than stopping at the first complete match. Normally, this characteristic doesn't matter too much, but when you combine wildcards with repetition operators you can wind up grabbing more than you expect.

Consider the following example. If we have a regular expression like `a.*b` that says we want to find an a followed by any number of characters up to a b, then the match function will search from the first a to the *last* b. That is, if the searched string includes more than one b all but the last one will be included in the `.*` part of the expression. In the following example,

```
re.match('a.*b','abracadabra')
```

the MatchObject matches all of `abracadab`—not just the first b. Failing to anticipate this greedy matching behavior is one of the most common errors made by new users of regular expressions.

To prevent this greedy behavior, simply add a `?` after the repetition character, like so:

```
re.match('a.*?b','abracadabra')
```

This code will now match only `ab`.

Conditionals

The final piece in the jigsaw puzzle is to make the regular expression search for optional elements or to select one of several patterns. We'll look at each of these options separately.

Optional Elements

You can specify that a character is optional by using zero or more repetition meta-characters.

```
>>> re.match('computer?d?', 'computer')
<re.MatchObject instance at 864890>
```

The preceding code will match `computer` or `computed`. It will also match `computerd`, which we don't want.

By using a range within the expression, we can be more specific.

```
>>> re.match('compute[rd]','computer')
<re.MatchObject instance at 874390>
```

This code will select `computer` and `computed` but reject the unwanted `computerd`.

Optional Expressions

In addition to matching options from a list of characters, we can match based on a choice of subexpressions. As mentioned earlier, we can group sequences of characters in parentheses. In fact, we can group any arbitrary regular expression in parentheses and treat it as a unit. In describing the syntax, we will use the notation `(RE)` to indicate any such regular expression grouping.

The situation we will examine here is the case in which we want to match a regular expression containing `(RE)xxxx` *or* `(RE)yyyy`, where `xxxx` and `yyyy` are different patterns. For example, we want to match both `premature` and `preventive`. We can do so by using a selection meta-character:

```
>>> regexp = 'pre(mature|ventive)'
>>> re.match(regexp,'premature')
<re.MatchObject instance at 864890>
>>> re.match(regexp,'preventive')
```

```
<re.MatchObject instance at 864890>
>>> re.match(regexp,'prelude')
```

Notice that when defining the regular expression we had to include both the options inside the parentheses. Otherwise, the option would have been restricted to `prematureentive` or `prematurventive`. In other words, only the letters "e" and "v" would have formed the options—not the groups.

Using Regular Expressions in Python

We've seen a little of what regular expressions look like, but now some questions arise: What can we do with them? And how do we do it in Python? To take the first point first, we can use regular expressions as very powerful search tools in text. We can look for lots of different variations of text strings in a single operation; we can even search for nonprintable characters such as blank lines by using some of the meta-characters. In addition, we can replace these patterns using the methods and functions of the **re** module. We've already seen the **match()** function at work, but several other functions are also available (Table 19-3).

	Function/Method	Effect
Table 19-3 re Module functions and methods	`match(RE,string)`	If RE matches the start of the `string`, it returns a MatchObject
	`search(RE,string)`	If RE is found anywhere within the `string` it returns a MatchObject
	`split(RE, string)`	Like `string.split()`, but uses RE as a separator
	`sub(RE, replace, string)`	Returns a string produced by substituting `replace` for RE at the first matching occurrence of RE. (This function has several additional features; see the documentation for details.)
	`compile(RE)`	Produces a regular expression *object* that can be reused for multiple operations with the same RE; the object has all of the methods listed in this table but with an implied RE and greater efficiency than the function versions.

Table 19-3 is not a comprehensive list of **re**'s methods and functions. Indeed, some of the functions and methods listed have optional parameters that can extend their use. The listed functions are the most commonly used operations and are sufficient for most needs.

To see how we might use regular expressions in Python, let's create a program that will search an HTML file for an IMG tag that has no ALT[2] section. If we find one, we will add a message to the owner to create more user-friendly HTML in the future!

```
import re
# detect "IMG" in upper/lowercase, allowing for
# zero or more spaces between the < and the "I"
img = '< *[iI][mM][gG] '
# allow any character up to the "ALT" or "alt" before >
alt = img + '.*[aA][lL][tT].*>'

# open file and read it into list
filename = raw_input('Enter a filename to search ')
inf = open(filename,'r')
lines = inf.readlines()

# if the line has an IMG tag and no ALT inside
# add our message as an HTML comment
for i in range(len(lines)):
    if re.search(img,lines[i]) and not \
        re.search(alt,lines[i]):
        lines[i] = '<!-- PROVIDE ALT TAGS ON IMAGES! -->\n' \
                    + lines[i]

# write the altered file and tidy up
inf.close()
outf = open(filename,'w')
outf.writelines(lines)
outf.close()
```

---

2. The IMG tag in HTML adds an image to the page. The ALT tag provides an alternative text so that if the browser cannot display images or has images switched off (perhaps to increase download speed), then the user sees a description of the image and thereby gains some idea of how the page would look if the image was present. Even on browsers that display images, the ALT tag is useful because the browser will display the ALT text as a ToolTip when the mouse is held over the image. In short, you should always provide an ALT tag when adding images to HTML pages.

Notice two points about this code. First, we use `re.search` instead of `re.match`, because `search` finds the patterns anywhere in the string whereas `match` looks only at the start of the string. Second, we use a statement continuation character, "\", in the `if` statements. This choice allows us to lay the code out over two lines, which looks a little neater, especially if many expressions will be combined.

This code is far from perfect, because it doesn't consider the case where the IMG tag may be split over several lines. Nevertheless, it illustrates the technique well enough for our purposes. Of course, such wanton vandalism of HTML files shouldn't really be encouraged. Then again, anyone who doesn't provide ALT tags probably deserves all they get!

We'll see regular expressions at work again in the case studies. In the meantime, experiment with them and check out the other methods in the `re` module. We have merely scratched the surface of what's possible using these powerful text-processing tools.

Points to Remember

Regular expressions are used to match text patterns.

Meta-characters are used to indicate position, repetition, and optionality of characters or groups.

Python's `re` module provides powerful tools for working with regular expressions.

---

3. *This name apparently comes from the original UNIX line editor, ed, which had a g/re/p command that had the same effect as the grep command. It printed out all lines in a file that contained the regular expression re. Other sources state that grep stands for General Regular Expression Parser. Whichever is correct, grep is not as strangely named as it may seem on first acquaintance.*

Chapter
20 Debugging

What will we cover?

- *A process for debugging*

- *Use of* pdb, *the Python debugger*

- *General hints about debugging techniques and likely causes of faults*

Stop, Look, and Think

In any nontrivial program, occasions will arise when things don't work quite as you expect. This situation can prompt any of several responses. For example, you might be tempted to jump in and start changing the code, almost at random, in the hope that you can fix it. This approach usually leads to chaos and a program that no one can understand. Resist that temptation at all costs! Another potential response is to ditch the entire program and start again. This tactic offers no guarantee of success and is usually unnecessary, because the problem will often turn out to be something very simple. The best method of dealing with problems in code is to stop, take a deep breath, and think about what is happening, what should be happening, and why the two don't match.

Having thought about the possible reasons for the fault, you can then narrow down the search by using a number of techniques, all of which come under the general banner of *debugging*. Debugging simply means the process of finding bugs, or errors, in your code. There is nothing very mysterious about it. If approached with the right attitude it can even be an enjoyable part of the programming experience!

During the analysis stage of debugging, consider some of the likely causes of problems:

- Am I trying to open a nonexistent file? Or a file with no content?

- Have I inadvertently included a statement in a loop that should really be outside the loop? Reinitializing a loop counter to zero inside a `while` loop rather than before it, which produces an infinite loop, is a common example of this problem.

- Have I initialized all of my variables? This problem is more common in languages like C or Java than it is in Python, which requires some kind of initialization to create a variable. Even in Python, it's possible to create a variable with an empty list or dictionary when you really meant to populate it with 0 or some other initial value.

- Are my Boolean conditions reversed? It's amazingly easy to test for ">" instead of "<". Also, consider whether you should be using an equality check—for example, ">=" rather than ">".

If all of these things are okay, then we can progress to the next stage of debugging: printing out key information as the program runs.

Print

We've been using `print` all the way through the book, and this method really is a very useful tool. You can print just about anything in Python and get a reasonably meaningful response. Thus, just by sprinkling `print` statements throughout your program at critical points, you can examine the states of your key variables and structures.

Let's consider an example. When I was writing Chapter 15 on recursion, I accidentally missed the multiplication in the last line of the `factorial()` function. As a result, the function always returned 1. In that case, I had just explained in the text how it should work. By applying *stop, look, and think* techniques, I easily spotted the problem and fixed it. Now let's assume that I was being particularly slow and didn't spot the problem. Let's see how I could have found the fault using `print` statements.

The faulty code looked like this:

```
def factorial(N):
    if N <= 1: return 1
    else: return factorial(N-1)
```

Because of the structure of the code, it's actually quite difficult to print anything except N, which doesn't really help us very much. First, we need to open up the code a little by adding some *scaffolding*, or temporary code intended to help us test or debug the program:

```
def factorial(N):
    print 'N= ',N
    if N <= 1: retval = 1
    else: retval = factorial(N-1)
    print 'retval = ', retval
    return retval
```

Now when we run the program, we can see the input and output values each time the factorial function is called, which is much more useful. It looks like this:

```
>>> from factorial import factorial
>>> factorial(3)
N= 3
N= 2
N= 1
retval = 1
retval = 1
retval = 1
1
```

This result immediately draws our attention to the return value as being faulty. We should now be able to figure out how we can fix it. In this case, we need to multiply retval by N. Removing our print statements and scaffolding, we get the final working version:

```
def factorial(N):
    if N <= 1: return 1
    else: return N * factorial(N-1)
```

Other good strategies for using print include printing out the names of functions as you enter them along with their parameter values. Similarly, putting a print statement into each __init__() method of classes lets us see what objects we are creating as a program runs.

Many professional programmers rarely use anything other than simple print statements to debug their code. The only caveat is that you must remember to remove the scaffolding (or comment it out) when you're done.

The Python Debugger

If thought and use of print statements are still not enough to solve the problem, then it's time to wheel out the heavy artillery of bug hunting. Python comes with a debugging tool in the form of the pdb module. This text-based tool is modeled on the well-known gdb debugger used for many years on UNIX systems for debugging C code. We'll look at the commands available in the command-prompt version of pdb and then conclude by illustrating IDLE's debug tools, which are built on top of pdb.

Starting the Debugger

To start pdb, you must first import the pdb module and then issue the run command:

```
>>> import pdb
>>> pdb.run(1)
> E:\Python\Lib\exceptions.py(65)__init__()
-> def __init__(self, *args):
(pdb)
```

We can now type commands at the pdb prompt. The first command to try is probably help, which provides a list of the available commands. Typing help <command> will provide more detailed help on each command:

```
(pdb) help
Documented commands (type help <topic>):
==========================================
```

EOF	a	alias	args	b
break	c	cl	clear	condition
cont	continue	d	disable	down
enable	h	help	ignore	l
list	n	next	p	q

```
quit         r          return        s step
tbreak       u          unalias       up w
whatis       where
Miscellaneous help topics:
===========================
pdb               exec
Undocumented commands:
======================
retval            rv
```

Many of the commands listed are just shortcuts for the full version; for example, h is a short-cut for help. Try asking for help on a few of the commands. You'll see that the help is fairly terse but usually sufficient to tell you what the command does.

To exit pdb, type q or quit.

Stepping Through the Code

To debug our program, assuming it is in a separate module, we can use pdb's run command. Let's repeat our debug exercise on the factorial function, this time using pdb:

```
>>> import pdb
>>> import factorial
>>> pdb.run('factorial.factorial(3)')# enclose command in ''
> <string>(0)?()->None
(pdb)
```

We're now in the debugger, and pdb is waiting for us to tell it what to do next. One foible of pdb is that it usually stops a couple of steps away from the place you expect it to be. In that case, just hit s (for step) a few times until you see your code appear.

```
(pdb) s
> <string>(1)?()->None
(pdb) s
> E:\PROJECTS\PYTHON\factorial.py(1)factorial()
-> def factorial(n):
(pdb)
```

We've reached the first line of our function. It might be a good idea to list the code, just to remind ourselves what it looks like:

```
(pdb) list
  1    ->def factorial(n):
  2             if n <= 1:
  3                  return 1
  4             else:
  5             return factorial(n-1)
  6
  7  if __name__ == "__main__":
  8             from sys import argv
  9         if len(argv) > 1:
 10             print factorial(eval(argv[1]))
 11
(Pdb)
```

That looks okay, so let's check the value of n using the print (p) command:

```
(pdb) p n
3
(pdb)
```

That's okay, too. Now we'll step through the function, checking n at intervals:

```
(pdb) s
> E:\PROJECTS\PYTHON\factorial.py(2)factorial()
-> if n <= 1:
(pdb) s
> E:\PROJECTS\PYTHON\factorial.py(5)factorial()
-> return factorial(n-1)
(pdb) s
> E:\PROJECTS\PYTHON\factorial.py(1)factorial()
-> def factorial(n):
(pdb) p n              # now inside recursive call to factorial
2
```

```
(pdb) s
> E:\PROJECTS\PYTHON\factorial.py(2)factorial()
-> if n <= 1:
(pdb) s
> E:\PROJECTS\PYTHON\factorial.py(5)factorial()
-> return factorial(n-1)
(pdb) s
> E:\PROJECTS\PYTHON\factorial.py(1)factorial()
-> def factorial(n):
(pdb) p n
1
(pdb) s
> E:\PROJECTS\PYTHON\factorial.py(2)factorial()
-> if n <= 1:
(pdb) s
> E:\PROJECTS\PYTHON\factorial.py(3)factorial()
-> return 1
(pdb) s
--Return--
> E:\PROJECTS\PYTHON\factorial.py(3)factorial()->1
-> return 1
(pdb)
```

We can see the problem with repeated return 1's appearing. Looking at the return statement in the source code, we see that we're missing the multiplier. We can easily fix this problem.

Another Use for the Debugger

Stepping through code one line at a time is extremely tedious, but it can be a very effective way of getting to know a new program if you don't have any other documentation. One of my colleagues once spent an entire week doing nothing but stepping through a large C program that he had "inherited" with no documentation other than a user manual. At the end of the week, he had visited just about every nook and cranny of the code and had drawn some diagrams to show how it all hung together. This exercise was much faster and more effective that just reading the code listing would have been.

Breakpoints

Normally it's not necessary to step through the entire program. In most cases, you'll have a rough idea of where the problem lies, especially if you've already tried putting in some `print` statements, as suggested earlier. If you are writing an event-driven program, stepping through the code may not even be an option because control will pass back to the event loop, which is probably part of the operating system! How can we handle these situations?

Fortunately, pdb provides a mechanism for running the program at full speed until it reaches a place in which we have registered an interest. This process of telling the debugger to stop the program at a particular location is known as setting a *breakpoint*.

To demonstrate the use of breakpoints, we'll create a small test module, which we'll call `foobar.py`. This module contains a bug:

```
def foo(num):
    print num*2


def bar(n):
    for i in range(n):
        foo(n)
```

Let's run the program:

```
>>> import foobar
>>> bar(4)
8
8
8
8
```

We were expecting to get `0,2,4,6`. Let's start the Python interactive prompt and debug our module:[1]

```
>>> import pdb
>>> import foobar
>>> pdb.run('foobar.bar(4)')
> <string>(0)?()->None
(pdb)
```

---

1. Note that we haven't stopped to think about the possible cause or used `print` statements. That's because we're only illustrating how breakpoints work! Normally, you probably wouldn't need the debugger for such a small program.

We're now ready to start debugging. Let's set the breakpoint at foo(), which handles the printing. We use the b (or break) command:

```
(pdb) b foobar.foo
Breakpoint 4 at E:\PROJECTS\PYTHON\foobar.py:2
(pdb)
```

We've set a breakpoint at foo[2] and can now use the c (or cont) command to continue execution until we reach our breakpoint at the start of foo():

```
(pdb) c
> <string>(1)?()->None
(pdb) c
> E:\PROJECTS\PYTHON\foobar.py(2)foo()
-> print num * 2
(pdb)
```

We've stopped at a line of code. Let's see the context using the list command, limiting the output to only the first five lines:

```
(pdb) l 1,5
  1     def foo(num):
  2 B->     print num * 2
  3
  4     def bar(n):
  5         for i in range(n):
(pdb)
```

A B indicates where a breakpoint has been set, and a -> sign indicates where pdb has stopped: the first line of foo(). Now we can examine the values using pdb's print command:

```
(pdb) p num
4
```

---

2. We don't use parentheses after foo, because we are telling Python to stop at the foo function object.

That's wrong. We expected to get 0 here, not 4. Let's move up a level and see why we've received the wrong value.

```
(pdb) up
> E:\PROJECTS\PYTHON\foobar.py(6)bar()
-> foo(n)
(pdb) l
    1     def foo(num):
    2 B       print num * 2
    3
    4     def bar(n):
    5         for i in range(n):
    6  ->          foo(n)
    7
[EOF]
(pdb)
```

We are now one level higher in the call stack—namely, inside bar() at the point where it calls foo(). Let's look at the variable values here.

```
(pdb) p i
0
(pdb) p n
4
(pdb)
```

It's fairly obvious that we are passing n into foo() rather than i, which explains why we get the same result each time. That problem is easy to fix. We can readily make the change and move on to our next challenge, whatever it may be.

Debugging in IDLE

IDLE actually comes with a GUI debugging tool that acts as a front end to pdb. We can therefore perform most of the operations mentioned earlier[3] using point-and-click techniques. Figure 20-1 shows a screenshot of IDLE debugging the foobar module. Notice the three separate windows. The top

---

3. *The Pythonwin IDE has more sophisticated debugging support than IDLE but, as previously mentioned, is only available on Windows.*

window is the debugger, showing the current line and, in the bottom section, the values of i and n. The middle window is our source listing. The bottom window is the Python shell window, showing the output so far.

Figure 20-1
IDLE debugging the foobar module

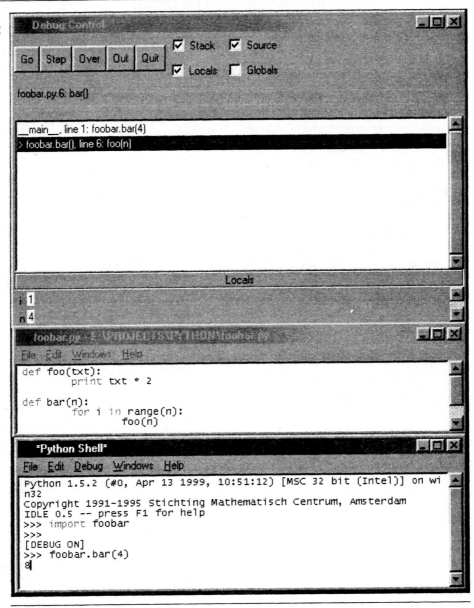

Some Additional Thoughts

This chapter has merely touched on the subject of debugging code. Much more can be covered, including the advanced use of `print` statements and the use of the debugger as a test harness. We also ignored the ability to set variables or execute arbitrary code segments within pdb. The reason for those omissions is that Python rarely requires that level of sophistication. If you follow the guidelines discussed earlier, you can usually figure out what's gone wrong fairly quickly. With other languages, the advanced use of a debugging tool may be an essential skill. You should therefore study the relevant documentation closely.

Things to Ponder

What kinds of mistakes have you made in the programs you've written so far? Is there a trend? Very often programmers develop their own particular bad habits. Knowing your own makes finding those bugs just a little bit easier!

Some leading lights in software engineering don't like the term "debugging." They think that the term "bug" is a bit too friendly and encourages programmers to treat bugs too lightly. They would prefer to use "error" or "fault". Do you feel that thinking you were "repairing faults" or "fixing errors" rather than "finding bugs" would make you treat the process differently?

We conclude with some general tips on debugging:

1. Consider turning off exceptions while debugging. They can prevent stack traces, which provide lots of useful debugging information.

2. Read Python error messages carefully. These messages, although initially cryptic, do contain most of the information you need to find the vast majority of errors in Python programs.

3. Use the Python interactive prompt to experiment with the faulty object or function. You can learn a great deal just by examining the behavior and comparing it with expected results.

4. Beware of boundary conditions. These conditions consist of the first and last items of lists and other structures. It's amazing how often they are missed by accident. Or perhaps you attempt to process an extra element past the boundary condition, by using a while loop to process up to len() instead of up to len()-1.

5. Don't jump into a pdb session too quickly. At the same time don't spend too much time inserting print statements. If a few judiciously chosen print statements don't reveal a pattern, then it's probably time to run up the debugger.

6. Most debugging techniques alter the original code. If your code is time-critical, then the debugging techniques may actually change the way your code behaves and introduce new bugs. If that's the case, strip out all but the minimum of scaffolding and use as few breakpoints as possible.

Points to Remember

Don't panic when bugs strike. Stop and think what the likely cause might be.

Bugs are faults that programmers create—they don't "just happen."

Carefully placed `print` *statements can show the state and flow of your program.*

Debugging tools allow you to step through your program line by line. Breakpoints allow you to zoom in on a target section of code quickly.

Use breakpoints to debug event-driven code such as GUIs. Set a breakpoint on the event handler, then stimulate the event so that the handler is called.

Read error messages carefully; they contain much useful information.

Chapter
21 Designing a Solution

What will we cover?

- *Putting together a larger project*

- *The development life cycle and techniques for dealing with it*

Once you know the basics of programming, you are ready to tackle some projects. Smaller projects are usually not too much of a problem, because you can keep the ideas and design all in your head. In most cases, you are building these projects for your own use, so you know exactly what's required. Once word gets out that you can program, however, other people suggest projects. It's here that many beginners get stuck, because it's much more difficult to program for someone else than for yourself. The other problem scenario arises where the program grows much larger than you anticipated; it can prove challenging to keep track of how it's all supposed to fit together. This chapter provides some pointers on how you might approach these types of projects.

Although the process is presented here as a sequence of steps, you don't need to follow the sequence exactly. For example, you need not wait until you have captured every requirement before you start the design phase. Once you understand one area (perhaps the data or user interface), you can begin to design and even build that part of the system. Similarly, don't wait to test the system until it's completely finished. Instead, test each component, class, and even function as you go, as it will make the final testing and validation go more smoothly.

Understand the Problem

The greatest challenge on any project is understanding what the program is supposed to do. When it's your own project, you just *know*. When the project is being developed for other people, their idea of what they want and your understanding of what they want can be radically different. To handle this issue, we have to introduce some techniques from the world of *software engineering*. Software engineering is the technical name for industrial-strength programming. It aims to provide a framework for producing programs that meet the requirements in a predictable and repeatable manner. Theories and methodologies abound regarding software engineering, but there are also some simple techniques that you can apply even on the smaller-scale projects that you are likely to encounter.

Statement of Requirements

The most important piece of information in any software project is the *statement of requirements*. This agreement between the programmer and the *customer* or *user* states *what* the program should do. It can be a fairly brief description—perhaps an e-mail or one-page memo. Nevertheless, it must describe as succinctly and as completely as possible what the program must do. One common way to capture these requirements is using a technique called *use cases*—that is, story boards of how the system will be used. Each major function of the system as envisaged by the user is documented either as a paragraph of text or more formally as a bullet list of steps. This technique can be as formal or informal as you choose to make it. Entire books have been written on the subject! The important thing is that your statement of requirements should provide a complete, testable description of the externals of the system.

Nonfunctional Requirements

Nonfunctional requirements are the bits that users usually forget to specify, but complain about bitterly when they don't get them—things like performance, look and feel, cost, memory, and CPU usage. As a programmer, it's your job to ask the questions that ensure that you capture those requirements and that they are realistic. I have seen more projects fail because the nonfunctional aspects didn't live up to expectations than for any other single reason.

Prioritization and Scope

With the best will in the world, you may not be able to develop all of the requirements within the budget and time constraints specified by the customer. In such a case, it's essential to get the requirements prioritized. Often 20% of the functionality can deliver 80% of the benefits. Make sure you understand which bits of the system offer the real benefits and build them first. If you can offer those components on time, the customer will probably be happy (or at least happier!). On the other hand, if you deliver the 80% that gives 20% benefit and omit the really important parts, you may have blackened your name forever.

Consider the Options

Once you know *what* to build, you need to decide *where* to build it. Among your first decisions will be a choice of operating system, programming language, and, if necessary, database. Will the program require a GUI or is a batch mode program sufficient? There are lots of options from which to choose, and the customer may have mandated much of it in the nonfunctional requirements—all her computers may be Apple Macs, for example.

Choose the Tools

Once the basic architecture of the system is settled, you need to select your language and possibly the toolset. Normally you, as a programmer, will have full control here—so think about what is most appropriate for the job. Appendix B compares several languages, providing some guidance as to the kinds of tasks to which they are best suited. If you don't know a particular language, however, you must offset the time lost learning it against the time gained using it. The same applies to tools. If you have to learn a new editor or debugger, it can slow you down even more than learning a new language!

Static versus Dynamic Design

Having worked out the requirements for the project—*what* you need to build—it's now time to think about design—*how* you will build it. Design is typically split into dynamic and static design. Static design involves the structure of the data or objects, their relationships, inheritance structure, and similar issues.

Dynamic design focuses on the interaction between the components, messages between objects, function call hierarchy, and so on. You don't really know how the system will work until you've thought about both aspects.

Data or Objects

If your project primarily manipulates data stored in flat files or an existing database, you may want to start your design by working out exactly which bits of data you will need and how they relate to each other and to the project requirements. If your project is more process-oriented or functional in nature, you may find it easier to think about which classes and objects you will need and how they will interact. Using that analysis, you can then create a list of the data items to be stored. The choice is yours.

When dealing with objects, a key principle to bear in mind is that objects (and by implication their classes) have *responsibilities*. Deciding on a class's responsibilities is by far the most important part of object-oriented design. The responsibilities will then determine what data each object needs to contain to manage those responsibilities.

A related principle is that objects should "do it to themselves." If you find yourself asking one object, A, for a reference to a second object, B, so that you can send B a message, you should ask why A isn't doing the work for you, as A has taken on the responsibility for managing B by virtue of holding a reference to it. This strategy may simply involve A passing the message directly to B (known as *delegating*). Similarly, if you find yourself sending a sequence of messages to a single object with no other processing in between, then it suggests that a method is missing from the receiving object—it should have a means of handling the subsidiary messaging to itself in response to a single message from you.

Finally, don't overdo an object's responsibilities. It can be tempting to have a method do more than its fair share just because it is already involved in a transaction. An object should live up to its own responsibilities, but do no more than that.

Timing and Synchronization

Timing and synchronization are important aspects of many programs, especially those involving communications with hardware, whether it be connecting to a network or just reading the keyboard. If your program is batch-oriented but has some kind of interaction, possibly with a user, consider how you will respond to external events that occur during periods of heavy processing. If your program is event-driven, consider how you will handle events that don't arrive in the expected sequence.

Working within Your Environment

Every programming environment imposes its own set of constraints upon you as a programmer. It is important that you understand what these restrictions are and how you can live with them. For example, Python restricts our low-level access to the operating system and our ability to create very-high-speed, graphics-intensive games such as Quake. Most of the operating system features are available to us via libraries and modules, however, and interfaces to high-speed graphics libraries can be used, so it is only in extreme situations that we need feel limited by the language. In those specific cases, we must accept the limitation or change to a different language—which will inevitably have limitations of its own. There is no perfect language!

Operating System Constraints

Sometimes the restrictions reflect the operating system itself rather than the programming environment. For example, MS-DOS does not readily support multitasking (running several programs at the same time) or offer support for multiple users. Other operating systems may not offer support for reacting to hardware interrupts in a prompt manner and so be unsuitable for building time-critical systems.[1] The important point is not to become frustrated by these limitations, but rather to recognize and accept that they exist in one form or another on every platform. Work with the system as far as you can, work around it where you can, and accept the rest. It will lead to a more relaxed life!

Integration with Existing Systems

When your program must communicate with other systems, you will often find that the operational environment imposes restrictions on your design. Most commonly, this communication is likely to involve an existing database from which you need to extract information. It could, however, be a piece of hardware or a network connection to another computer.[2] The important point is that you must discover what the *interface* looks like. In the case of a database, it is likely to use some variant of the Structured Query Language (SQL, pronounced "sequel"). For hardware, there will likely be an application programming interface (API). Networks tend to use well-defined protocols such

---

1. *A family of real-time operating systems has been developed specifically for this type of application area, including QNX, VxWorks, RTOS, and OS-9. Unless you decide to become a full-time programming professional, you're unlikely to be working with any of these operating systems. The exception may be an electronics enthusiast who is building his or her own hardware and writing the software to control it.*
2. *This type of interaction is becoming increasingly common with the rise of Internet and Web-based applications.*

as TCP/IP. In each case, you must obtain documentation of some sort and create a set of functions or a class that allows your code to communicate with the other system.[3]

Testing

Testing is an essential part of any project. On informal projects for your own benefit, you will test the program yourself, often by using it and fixing things as they go wrong. That approach isn't practical if you intend to ship the program to lots of users. In that situation, you will need to set up a rigorous testing phase to check every feature of the program. This is where capturing your requirements, especially as use cases, really helps. You will already have a complete list of what needs to be tested in your statement of requirements.

If possible, you should have someone else test your program. It is very hard for a programmer to really try to break his or her own code. The programmer has a built-in knowledge of how it should work and a reluctance to do "stupid" things that an end user will have no hesitation in attempting! Likewise, an independent tester will not hesitate to use strange and bizarre ways to find faults. The important thing for you as a programmer is to recognize that this effort is a good thing and to not argue with the tester. If a tester can find the fault, sooner or later a user will.

Configuration Management

Configuration management (CM) has been described as the ability to do a "collective undo." It focuses on recovering old versions of your software, either a single file or the entire project. When working as an individual programmer, you might find a simple file compression/archiving tool is sufficient: use Zip or a similar utility to archive the working project files and save the compressed collection to a safe place, such as a backup disk, floppy, or CD-ROM. If you later need to revert to the previous version—perhaps to fix bugs reported by users—you can simply recreate the project from the Zip file. This type of CM is often known as *release management* and is essential on any project that you are deploying to other users.

---

3. *A significant part of my experience has been in getting different systems to communicate. I rather enjoy this kind of programming. Some of my colleagues refer to it using the disparaging description of "plumbing." Different strokes for different folks, I guess!*

Things to Ponder

How similar is software engineering to other types of engineering? Are there any fundamental differences?

Much debate has arisen regarding how detailed a design should be. Some think that defining only classes and some key methods is adequate; others like to produce pseudocode for every method or function. What level do you think would be best? Are there circumstances where your answer might change?

The open source ethos of software development on the Internet has received much publicity recently. It often relies on large, very widely dispersed teams who often don't know each other very well. What additional challenges would result from working on such a project?

The other type of CM, which is known as *version management* or *version control* focuses on controlling individual files. It goes hand in hand with release management, because to do the latter you must to some degree do the former. Most people use tools to do version control, and several good freeware or shareware tools are readily available. In addition, commercial packages range in price from a few hundred dollars to hundreds of thousands of dollars. The system that is most likely to appeal to readers of this book is both free and easy to use but nonetheless quite capable of managing fairly sophisticated projects. It's called GNU RCS (Revision Control System) and is available for most computer platforms. Once you have it installed, everyday use involves creating a subdirectory in your project directory called RCS and then issuing ci and co commands to check your files *in* or *out*. If you specify a -l option, then the file will be *locked* so that no one else can change the file until you have checked it in. This approach helps to prevent one programmer from overwriting changes made by another programmer.

RCS will prompt you for a brief description of the file when you first check it in and for a reason for the change after every update. These comments can be automatically placed in the header of your file by putting the special symbol $log in the file. RCS replaces the $log with the history that it has recorded.

The individual programmer can also use RCS during prototyping as a very simple way of keeping track of the changes—thus every prototype that works can be frozen. If later versions stop working, you can instantly revert to a previous version by using the co command with a -r flag and providing a *revision number*.

RCS has lots of other facilities and comes with full documentation. I strongly recommend that you give it a try.

Points to Remember

Make sure you understand the requirements—what you are trying to build.

Keep designs as simple as possible, but do not force a single component to do more than it should.

Document your interfaces, especially if you are working as part of a team.

Consider both the dynamic aspects of the design and the static relationships between objects. Think about the physical design in terms of modules and your plan to deploy and install the finished system.

Use configuration management to keep control of old releases and version control to manage individual files during the production stage (preventing overwriting of files, for example).

Section 4

Case Studies

In this section we look at two case studies. In Chapter 22, we extend the word counter example introduced in Section 2; in Chapter 23, we provide an object-oriented framework for writing guessing games. The purpose of the case studies is not to create polished, professional-standard programs but rather to illustrate the process of taking an idea and developing the code necessary for a working program. The examples are intended to demonstrate the kind of programs that a reader of this book should be able to create for himself or herself with a little thought and effort.

Chapter

22

Grammar Counter

What will we cover?

- *Improving the word counter to handle lines and characters*
- *Extending the word counter to count punctuation and grammatical features*
- *Turning it into an object-based solution*
- *Converting the grammar counter into a GUI-based tool*

In this case study, we expand the word-counting program developed earlier in this book. We will create a program that mimics the UNIX wc program in that it outputs the number of lines, words, and characters in a file. We will go further than that, however, and also output the number of sentences, clauses, words, letters, and punctuation characters in a text file. We will follow the development of this program stage by stage, gradually increasing its capability, then moving it into a module to make it reusable and finally turning it into an object-oriented implementation for maximum extendability and adding a GUI interface for ease of use.

Although the resulting program will be a Python implementation, mostly we want to focus on the process of developing the program in incremental steps. As we move to the more complex parts, we will make increasing use of Python's built-in data structures.

Counting Lines, Words, and Characters

Let's revisit the word counter program:

```
import string
def numwords(s):
    list = string.split(s)
    return len(list)

inp = open("menu.txt","r")
total = 0

# accumulate totals for each line
for line in inp.readlines():
    total = total + numwords(line)
print "File had %d words" % total

inp.close()
```

We need to add a line and character counter. The line count is easy to achieve: as we loop over each line, we just need a variable that is incremented on each iteration of the loop. The character count is only marginally more difficult to effect because we can find the length of each line and accumulate these lengths in yet another variable.

We also need to make the program more general, so that it reads the name of the file from the command line or, if this name is not provided, prompts the user for the name. An alternative strategy would be to read from standard input, which is what the real wc does.

The final word counter has the following form:

```
import sys, string

# Get the file name either from the command line or user
if len(sys.argv) < 2:
    name = raw_input('Enter the file name: ')
```

```
else:
    name = sys.argv[1]

inp = open(name,'r')

# initialize counters to zero, creating variables
words = 0
lines = 0
chars = 0

for line in inp.readlines():
    lines = lines + 1
    # break into a list of words and count them
    list = string.split(line)
    words = words + len(list)
    # count how many characters were in the line
    chars = chars + len(line)

fmtstr = "%s has %d lines, %d words and %d characters"
print fmtstr % (name, lines, words, chars)
inp.close()
```

If you are familiar with the UNIX wc command, you know that you can pass it a file name containing a wildcard to get statistics for all matching files as well as a grand total. This program handles only single file names. If you want to extend it to cater for wildcards, take a look at the glob module and build a list of names, then iterate over the file list. You'll need temporary counters for each file and cumulative counters for the grand totals. Or you could use a dictionary instead.

Counting Sentences

When I first thought about how we could extend this program to count sentences and words rather than "character groups," my initial idea was to loop through the file extracting the sentences into a list, loop through each sentence extracting the words into another list, and finally process each "word" to remove any extraneous characters.

If we simply collect the words and punctuation characters, however, we can analyze the latter to count sentences, clauses, and so on (by defining what we consider a sentence and clause in terms of punctuation items). Thus, we need to iterate over the file only once collecting punctuation and then iterate over the punctuation—a much smaller list. Let's try sketching that idea in pseudocode:

```
foreach line in file:
    increment line count
    if line empty:
        increment paragraph count
    split line into character groups

foreach character group:
    increment group count
    extract punctuation chars into a dictionary - {char:count}
    if no chars left:
        delete group
    else: increment word count

sentence count = sum of('.', '?', '!')
clause count = sum of all punctuation (very poor definition...)

report paras, lines, sentences, clauses, groups, words.
foreach punctuation char:
    report count
```

We could create perhaps four functions using the natural groupings in the pseudocode. This approach might help us build a module that could be reused either as a whole or in part.

Turning the Pseudocode into a Module

The key functions are getCharGroups(infile) and getPunctuation(wordList). Let's see what we come up with based
on the pseudocode.

```
############################
# Module: grammar
# Created: A.J. Gauld, 1999,8,19
#
# Function:
# Counts paragraphs, lines, sentences, 'clauses', chars,
# words, and punctuation for a prose-like text file.
# It assumes that sentences end with [.!?] and
# paragraphs have a blank line between them.
# A "clause" is simply a segment of sentence separated
# by punctuation (brain-dead but maybe someday we'll
# do better!)
#
# Usage: Takes a file name parameter and outputs all
#         stats. Its really intended that a second module
#         use the functions provided to produce more
#         useful commands.
############################
import string, sys
############################
# initialize global variables
para_count = 1 # assume at least one para exists!
line_count, sentence_count, clause_count, word_count = 0,0,0,0
groups = []
alphas = string.letters + string.digits
stop_tokens = ['.','?','!']
punctuation_chars = ['&','(',')','-',';',':',','] + \
                    stop_tokens
```

```
punctuation_counts = {}
for c in punctuation_chars:
    punctuation_counts[c] = 0
format = """%s contains:
%d paragraphs, %d lines and %d sentences.
These in turn contain %d clauses and a total of %d words."""


##############################
# Now define the functions that do the work
def getCharGroups(infile):
    pass


def getPunctuation(wordList):
    pass


def reportStats():
    print format % (sys.argv[1],
                    para_count, line_count, sentence_count,
                    clause_count, word_count)


def Analyze(infile):
    getCharGroups(infile)
    getPunctuation(groups)
    reportStats()


# make it run if called from the command line in which
# case the "magic" __name__ variable gets set to "__main__"
if __name__ == "__main__":
    if len(sys.argv) <> 2:
        print "Usage: python grammer.py < filename >"
        sys.exit()
    else:
        Document = open(sys.argv[1],"r")
        Analyze(Document)
```

Rather than trying to show the entire program in one long listing, let's examine this skeleton first and then consider each of the three significant functions in turn. Notice that the Python keyword pass signifies that there was no code to execute for these functions. This type of noneffective instruction is sometimes called a *no-op* or *nop*.[1] To make the program work, you must paste it all together at the end.

First, notice the comments at the top of the code. It is common practice to inform readers about what the file contains and how it should be used. The version information (author, revision, and date) is useful if you are comparing your results with those of someone who is using a more or less recent version; ideally, this information should be created automatically by our version control tool (See Chapter 21).

The final section uses a feature of Python that calls any module loaded at the command line __main__. We can test the built-in __name__ variable; therefore if it's __main__, we know the module is being run rather than imported. We therefore execute the trigger code inside the if statement. This trigger code includes a user-friendly hint about how the program should be run if no file name is provided or if too many file names are given.

Notice also that the Analyze() function calls the other functions in the right order. It is common practice to allow a programmer using the module to choose either to use all of the functionality in a straightforward manner (through Analyze()) or to call the low-level primitive functions directly.

getCharGroups()

The pseudocode for this segment follows:

```
foreach line in file:
    increment line count
    if line empty:
        increment paragraph count
    split line into character groups
```

---

1. NOP *is often the mnemonic used in assembler languages for an instruction that does nothing. In assembler programming, these instructions are usually used to fine-tune timing loops, in Python, they are used either as placeholders (as we are doing) or to create abstract methods in a class that expects subclasses to implement the real behavior.*

```
def trim(item, end=2):
    """ remove non alphas from left(0), right(-1) or
        both ends(2) of item"""

    if end not in [-1,0,2]:
        raise "InvalidEnd"
    if end == 2:
        trim(item,-1)       # first the right
        trim(item,0)        # then the left
    else:
        while (len(item) > 0) and (item[end] not in alphas):
            ch = item[end]
            if ch in punctuation_counts.keys():
                punctuation_counts[ch]=punctuation_counts[ch]+1
            if end == 0: item = item[1:]
            if end == -1: item = item[:-1]
```

Notice the use of recursion combined with default parameter values to create a single `trim` function that by default trims both ends; by passing in an end value, this function can be made to operate on only one end, however. The end values were chosen to be reminiscent of Python's indexing scheme. Originally, I wrote two separate trim functions. The amount of duplication in the code convinced me that I should be able to parameterize the code and create one general-purpose function instead. A bit of thought and the preceeding function was the result.

Completing `getPunctuation` becomes a nearly trivial task:

```
def getPunctuation(wordList):
    # strip punctuation from char groups
    for item in wordList:
        trim(item)                      # See Note 1
    # delete any empty "words"
    for i in range(len(wordList)):      # See Note 2
        if len(wordList[i]) == 0:
            del(wordList[i])
```

■ *Note 1:* The `trim` function is called in its default form, which strips nonletters from both ends.

■ *Note 2:* The code now deletes blank words.

The Final Grammar Module

The only task remaining is to improve the reporting to include the punctuation characters and the counts. We replace the existing `reportStats()` function with the following code:

```
def reportStats():
    global sentence_count, clause_count
    for p in stop_tokens:
        sentence_count = sentence_count + \
                            punctuation_counts[p]
    for c in punctuation_counts.keys():
        clause_count = clause_count + punctuation_counts[c]
    print format % (sys.argv[1],
            paragraph_count, line_count, sentence_count,
            clause_count, len(groups))
    print "The following punctuation characters were used:"
    for p in punctuation_counts.keys():
        print "\t%s\t:\t%3d" % (p, punctuation_counts[p])
```

If you have carefully stitched together all the functions, you should be able to type

```
C:> python grammar.py myfile.txt
```

and get a statistical report for `myfile.txt` (or whatever the file is really called). How useful this information is to you is debatable. Nevertheless, walking through the evolution of this code should have given you some idea of how to create your own programs. The main thing is to try things out. There's no shame in trying several approaches—often you learn very valuable lessons in the process.

In the next phase of our case study, we will rework the grammar module to use object-oriented techniques. In the process you will see how an object-oriented approach results in modules that are even more flexible for the user and more extensible.

Classes and Objects

A major problem for any programmer using our module is its reliance on global variables. As a consequence, the program can analyze only one document at a time. Any attempt to handle multiple documents will result in the global values being overwritten.

By moving these global variables into a class, we can create multiple instances of the class (one per file) and each instance will get its own set of variables. Furthermore, by making the methods sufficiently granular, we can create an architecture that makes it easy for the creator of a new type of document object to modify the search criteria to cater to the rules of the new type (for example, by rejecting all HTML tags from the word list). Our first attempt at this modification follows:

```
#! /usr/local/bin/python
###############################
# Module: document.py
# Author: A.J. Gauld
# Date:    1999/08/22
# Version: 0.1
###############################
# This module provides a Document class that
# can be subclassed for different categories of
# Document(text, HTML, Latex, etc.). Text and HTML are
# provided as samples.
#
# Primary services available include
#     - getCharGroups()
#     - getWords()
#     - reportStats()
###############################
import sys,string, re

class Document:
    def __init__(self, filename):
        self.filename = filename
        self.para_count = 1
```

```
        self.line_count, self.sentence_count = 0,0
        self.clause_count, self.word_count = 0,0
        self.alphas = string.letters + string.digits
        self.stop_tokens = ['.','?','!']
        self.punctuation_chars = ['&','(',')','-',
                                  ';',':',','] + \
                            self.stop_tokens
        self.punctuation_counts = {}
        self.groups = []
        for c in self.punctuation_chars:
            self.punctuation_counts[c] = 0
        self.format = """%s contains:
%d paragraphs, %d lines and %d sentences.
These in turn contain %d clauses and a total of %d words."""

    def getCharGroups(self):
        try:
            f = open(self.filename,"r")
            for line in f.readlines():
                self.line_count = self.line_count + 1
                if len(line) == 1: # only newline =>
                # para break
                    self.para_count = self.para_count + 1
                else:
                    self.groups = self.groups+string.split(line)
        except:
            print "Failed to read file", self.filename
            sys.exit()

    def getWords(self):
        pass

    def reportStats(self, paras=1,
                    lines=1, sentences=1,
                    words=1, punc=1):
        pass
```

```
def Analyze(self):
    self.getCharGroups()
    self.getWords()
    self.reportStats()

class TextDocument(Document):
    pass

class HTMLDocument(Document):
    pass

if __name__ == "__main__":
    if len(sys.argv) <> 2:
        print "Usage: python document.py "
        sys.exit()
    else:
        D = Document(sys.argv[1])
        D.Analyze()
```

To implement the `Document` class, we need to define the `getWords` method. We can simply copy what we did in the previous version and create a `trim` method that can trim either end or both ends if neccesary. In an object-oriented design that may not be the best approach, however, because to build classes that can be easily extended, we must provide *hooks* for use by other programmers who are creating new subclasses. Thus, if the designer of a new subclass of `Document` needed to trim a different set of characters from the left end than from the right end, our current function design would not support this task. It would be better to provide separate trim methods for each end.[2] This choice should allow a much wider scope for dealing with different types of documents.

Specifically, we will add methods to reject groups that we recognize as invalid and to trim unwanted characters from the left and from the right. We add these three methods to `Document` and implement `getWords` in terms of these methods.

---

2. *An alternative approach would be to make the existing* `trim` *method even more generic by passing in another parameter containing the list of valid characters. Either approach will work and provides the flexibility to extend the class without restriction.*

```
class Document:
    # .... as above
    def getWords(self):
        for i in range (len(self.groups)):
            self.groups[i] = self.ltrim(self.groups)
            self.groups[i] = self.rtrim(self.groups[i])
        self.removeExceptions()


    def removeExceptions(self):
        pass


    def ltrim(self,word):
        return word


    def rtrim(self,word):
        return word
```

Here we define the bodies to return their input with no change. If this behavior is required, it is available. In the more usual case, however, the subclass can change this behavior by overriding the methods.

Text Document

A text document is defined as follows:

```
class TextDocument(Document):
    def ltrim(self, word):
        while (len(word) > 0) and \
                (word[0] not in self.alphas):
            ch = word[0]
            if ch in self.punctuation_counts.keys():
                self.punctuation_counts[ch] = \
                                self.punctuation_counts[ch]+1
            word = word[1:]
        return word
```

```
def rtrim(self,word):
    while (len(word) > 0) and \
            (word[-1] not in self.alphas):
        ch = word[-1]
        if ch in self.punctuation_counts.keys():
            self.punctuation_counts[ch] = \
                        self.punctuation_counts[ch]+1
        word = word[:-1]
    return word


def removeExceptions(self):
    top = len(self.groups)
    i = 0
    while i < top:
        if (len(self.groups[i]) == 0):
            del(self.groups[i])
            top = top - 1
        i = i+1
```

The trim functions are slightly expanded versions of our grammar.py module's trim function, but with the parameterized parts replaced with dedicated indices. The removeExceptions function has been defined to remove blank words.

Notice that the structure of the removeExceptions function uses a while loop instead of a for loop. I originally used a for loop, but testing revealed a bug: if we deleted elements from the list, the range (which is calculated at the beginning) retained its original length and thus the program attempted to access members of the list beyond the end. To avoid that problem, I switched to a while loop and adjusted the maximum index each time an element was removed.

HTML Document

For HTML, we will take a very simplistic view and simply remove character groups beginning and ending with < and >. We will perform this task before we strip punctuation with ltrim and rtrim, so we need to redefine getWords. Regular expressions will help us identify the <...> tag patterns. The actual stripping of punctuation should work in the same way as for plain text. Consequently, instead of inheriting directly from Document, we will inherit from TextDocument and reuse its trim methods.

Thus the HTMLDocument class has the following form:

```
class HTMLDocument(TextDocument):
    def getCharGroups (self):
        tag = re.compile("<.+?>")
        para = re.compile("<[pP]>") # identify paragraph tags
        self.para_count = 0        # using <p>'s not empty lines
        f = open(self.filename, "r")   # should use try/except
        lines = f.readlines()
        n = 0
        while n < len (lines):
            if len(lines[n]) > 1:  # if its blank
                if para.search(lines[n]): # its not a paragraph
                    self.para_count = self.para_count + 1
                lines[n] = tag.sub('',lines[n]) # lose tags
                if len(lines[n]) <= 1: # empty or '\n' left
                    del(lines)[n]
                else:
                    self.groups=self.groups+string.split(lines[n])
                    n = n + 1
            else: n = n + 1
        self.line_count = len(lines)
```

Although using regular expressions in this way is much more powerful than using fixed strings to detect < or > it is still far from perfect. In particular, we will not correctly remove tags that span multiple lines and we are likely to make mistakes with nested tags such as these found within tables.

Adding a GUI

To create a GUI we will use Tkinter, which we introduced briefly in Chapter 18. This time the GUI will be slightly more sophisticated and use more of the graphical controls or *widgets* that Tkinter provides.

Refactoring the Document Class

Before we get to that stage, we need to modify our Document class. The current version prints the results to stdout as part of the Analyze method. For a GUI, we really don't want that behavior. Instead, we would like the Analyze method to store the totals in the counter attributes and allow us to access them as needed. We therefore split, or *refactor*, the reportStats() method into two parts: generateStats(), which will calculate the values and store them in the counters, and printStats(), which will print to stdout. As a general design principle, you should always separate the display and user interaction parts of a program from the processing and data manipulation parts.

Finally, we need to modify Analyze to call generateStats() and the main sequence to call printStats() after Analyze. With these changes in place, the existing code will carry on working as before, at least as far as the command-line user is concerned. Other programmers will have to make small changes to their code to call printStats() after using Analyze— not too onerous a task.

The revised code segments follow:

```
def generateStats(self):
    self.word_count = len(self.groups)
    for c in self.stop_tokens:
        sentence_count = sentence_count + \
                        self.punctuation_counts[c]
    for c in self.punctuation_counts.keys():
        clause_count = clause_count + \
                        self.punctuation_counts[c]


def printStats(self):
    print self.format % (self.filename, self.para_count,
                        self.line_count,
                         self.sentence_count,
                        self.clause_count,
                         self.words_count)
    print "The following punctuation characters were
    used:"
    for i in self.punctuation_counts.keys():
        print "\t%s\t:\t%4d" % \
                (i,self.punctuation_counts[i])
```

To make the module runnable, we add the following code:

```
if __name__ == "__main__":
    if len(sys.argv) <> 2:
        print "Usage: python document.py "
        sys.exit()
    else:
        try:
            D = HTMLDocument(sys.argv[1])
            D.Analyze()
            D.printStats()
        except:
            print "Error analyzing file: %s" % sys.argv[1]
```

Now we are ready to create a GUI wrapper around our document classes.

Designing a GUI

The first step in designing a GUI is to visualize how the end result will look. We need to specify a file name, so it will require an *Edit* or *Entry* control. We also need to specify whether we want textual or HTML analysis, a type of "one from many" choice that is usually represented by a set of *Radiobutton* controls. These controls should be grouped together to show that they are related.

The next requirement is for some kind of display of the results. We could opt for multiple *Label* controls, one per counter. Instead, let's use a simple *Text* control into which we can insert strings. This choice is closer to the spirit of the command-line output, although ultimately the choice is a matter of preference for the designer.

Finally, we need a means of initiating the analysis and quitting the application. Because we will be using a Text control to display results, it might be useful to have a means of resetting the display as well. These command options can all be represented by *Button* controls.

Sketching these ideas as a GUI gives us something like Figure 22-1.

Figure 22-1
Sketch of pro-
posed GUI for
grammar
counter

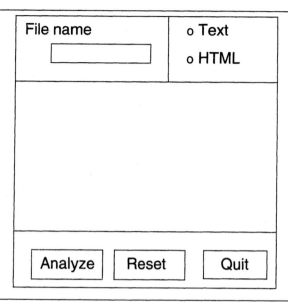

We arrange the individual controls into *frames,* which are just containers that allow us to keep related controls together. We then arrange the smaller frames into the overall frame, which is the application window. In this case, we have a frame containing the radio buttons combined with another frame for the file name entry and label. This combined frame is inserted into the top of the window. The text widget takes up the entire center space and therefore does not need to have its own containing frame. All of the buttons are contained with a single frame occupying the bottom of the window.

Tkinter Widgets

Tkinter provides a large selection of widgets for constructing GUIs. We will use only a small number of them here. Additional toolkits have been built on top of Tkinter to provide even more complex components should you find that Tkinter doesn't meet your needs. The best known of these added-value toolsets is Python MegaWidgets (PMW).

We will use the following widgets:

Frame: Container for other widgets. Frames can contain other frames ad infinitum.

Button: The most basic control. It has a caption and an associated command which is activated if the button is "pressed."

Entry: Single line text entry widget.

Text: Multiline text widget that can support multiple fonts, cut-and-paste, and embedded graphics.

Radiobutton: Choose any one out of many. It can be associated with a magic variable that automatically reflects the selected option (we use a more basic but generally applicable approach in the case study).

PhotoImage: Used in Chapter 23 to hold an image that is embedded in a Text control.

Now we can write some code. Let's take the process step by step:

```
from Tkinter import *
import document
```

```
############### CLASS DEFINITIONS ##################
class GrammarApp(Frame):
    def __init__(self, parent=0):
        Frame.__init__(self, parent)
        self.type = 2  # create a variable with default value
        self.master.title('Grammar counter')
        self.buildUI()
```

Here we have imported the Tkinter and document modules. For the former, we have made all of the Tkinter names visible within our current module. With the latter, we will need to prefix the names with "document."

We have also defined an __init__ method that calls the Frame.__init__ superclass method to ensure that Tkinter is set up properly internally. We then create an attribute that will store the document type value. Finally, we call the buildUI method, which creates the widgets for us.

```
    def buildUI(self):
        # the file information: File name and type
        fFile = Frame(self)
        Label(fFile, text="Filename: ").pack(side="left")
        self.eName = Entry(fFile)
        self.eName.insert(INSERT,"test.htm")
        self.eName.pack(side="left", padx=5)
```

```
# to keep the radio buttons lined up with the
# name we need another frame
fType = Frame(fFile, borderwidth=1, relief=SUNKEN)
self.rText = Radiobutton(fType, text="TEXT",
                         variable = self.type, value=2,
                         command=self.doText)
self.rText.pack(side=TOP)
self.rHTML = Radiobutton(fType, text="HTML",
                         variable=self.type, value=1,
                         command=self.doHTML)
self.rHTML.pack(side=TOP)
# make Text the default selection
self.rText.select()
fType.pack(side="right", padx=3)
fFile.pack(side="top", fill=X)


# the text box holds the output; pad gives a border
self.txtBox = Text(self, width=60, height=10)
self.txtBox.pack(side=TOP, padx=3, pady=3)


# use command buttons to do the real work
fButtons = Frame(self)
self.bAnalyze = Button(fButtons,
                       text="Analyze",
                       command=self.AnalyzeEvent)
self.bAnalyze.pack(side=LEFT, anchor=W, padx=50, pady=2)
self.bReset = Button(fButtons,
                     text="Reset",
                     command=self.doReset)
self.bReset.pack(side=LEFT, padx=10)
self.bQuit = Button(fButtons,
                    text="Quit",
                    command=self.doQuitEvent)
self.bQuit.pack(side=RIGHT, anchor=E, padx=50, pady=2)

fButtons.pack(side=BOTTOM, fill=X)
self.pack()
```

We will not examine all of this code in detail. Instead, you should take a look at the Tkinter tutorial found on the Python Web site. It offers an excellent introduction and reference to Tkinter. The general principle is that you create widgets from their corresponding classes, providing options as named parameters. The widget is then *packed* into its containing frame. Finally, we pack `self`, which is the top-level frame for the application.

Other key points to note are the use of subsidiary `Frame` widgets to hold the radio buttons and command buttons. The radio buttons also take a pair of options called `variable` and `value`. The former links the radio buttons together by specifying the same external variable (`self.type`), and the latter gives a unique value for each radio button.

Also notice the `command=xxx` options passed to the button controls. Tkinter will call these methods when the button is pressed. The code for these methods comes next:

```
#### EVENT-HANDLING METHODS ####
    # time to die...
    def doQuitEvent(self):
        import sys
        sys.exit()


    # restore default settings
    def doReset(self):
        self.txtBox.delete('1.0', END)
        self.rText.select()


    # set radio values
    def doText(self):
        self.type = 2


    def doHTML(self):
        self.type = 1
```

These methods are all fairly trivial and by now should be self explanatory to you. The Text widget's delete method takes an index string as a first parameter, in the form of "row.column". The first row is numbered 1 and the first column numbered 0. Hence `1.0` means from the beginning to the END.

The final event handler performs the analysis:

```
# Create appropriate document type and analyze it.
# then display the results in the form
    def AnalyzeEvent(self):
        filename = self.eName.get()
        if filename == "":
                self.txtBox.insert(END,"\nNo filename
                   provided!\n")
                return
        if self.type == 2:
                doc = document.TextDocument(filename)
        else:
                doc = document.HTMLDocument(filename)
        self.txtBox.insert(END, "\nAnalyzing...\n")
        doc.Analyze()
        str = doc.format % (filename,
                        doc.para_count, doc.line_count,
                        doc.sentence_count, doc.clause_count,
                        doc.word_count)
        self.txtBox.insert(END, str)
```

By now, you should be able to read this code and understand what it does. The key points are that it checks for a valid file name before creating the Document object and it uses the self.type value set by the radio buttons to determine which type of Document to create.

In addition, this code appends the results (the END argument to insert) to the Text box, so that we can analyze a document several times and compare results—one advantage of the Text box versus the multiple-label output approach.

All that's needed now is to create an instance of the GrammarApp class and set the event loop running. We use the following code:

```
myApp = GrammarApp()
myApp.mainloop()
```

Figure 22-2 shows the final result as seen under Microsoft Windows. It displays the results of analyzing a test HTML file, first in text mode and then in HTML mode.

Figure 22-2
Running the
grammar
counter
program

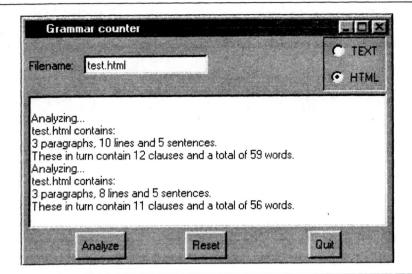

Several additional features could be implemented but will be left as exercises for the reader:

- Calculate the number of unique words used and their frequency

- Create a new version that analyzes RTF files

- Improve the HTML processing, perhaps by using the html modules in Python's standard library (You could, for example, list HTML tags and their frequency.)

If Tkinter has spurred your interest, you could try swapping the text box for multiple labels packed into a frame or even use a file picker dialog to populate the file name box. It's up to you how far you take this example—the only real limit is your imagination.

Things to Ponder

How useful is an application like the grammar counter? How could it be made more useful?

What other document types could be implemented? What sort of information would be needed?

Most GUIs have menus to control program function. Would a menu improve this application? Or would it just get in the way?

Points to Remember

Try to minimize the number of times you iterate over the data.

Try to separate display and processing parts of your programs.

Use frames to group components together within a GUI.

Chapter
23

Guessing Games

What will we cover?

- *Thinking about guessing games*

- *Building the prototype*

- *Creating a text-based Hangman game*

- *Converting to a GUI-based game*

- *Building a second game*

This chapter started out as a case study on building the popular game Hang-man. As the project progressed, it became obvious that Hangman is really just one manifestation of an entire category of games where the player must try to guess some word or pattern that an opponent (in our case, the computer) chooses. With that in mind, we will create a common framework that we could use to implement several versions of such games. Initially the discussion will focus on the original Hangman game, but as more general issues come to the fore we will discuss them as well. In essence, we will follow the evolution of the project more or less as it happened in practice.

The Game of Hangman

In case you haven't played this particular word game, let's review the rules and then think about what we need to do to write a version in Python. The objective in Hangman is to guess a word created by your opponent. At the start of the game, the word is represented as a series of blanks or underscores, one per letter. As you try to guess each letter, your opponent will either fill in the letters in the word or add a body part to a diagram of a hanging man on a scaffold. There are six body parts in total: the head, the trunk, two arms, and two legs. When the last body part is drawn, you lose that round. On the other hand, if you guess the word correctly before the drawing is complete, then you win.

That game sounds fairly easy and can be represented purely in text, which makes it easy for us to create a prototype. First, we need to create a valid word to guess. Thus we need a list of valid words (perhaps from a file) and a way of generating a random number to use as an index into the list. Having identified our word, we need some kind of representation that allows us to keep track of which letters have been guessed so that we can select letters correctly. Initially none of the letters will be guessed. We can read the guesses using raw_input. It's a nice touch to store the guesses and present them to the player as a reminder—and easily done with a simple list. To draw the hangman, we can use simple print statements and ASCII art. For the prototype, we'll just keep count of the mistakes and display how many body parts have been "drawn" so far. Part of a session might look something like the following output:

```
Word to guess: _____  You have 6 lives left
Type something: e
Word to guess: _____  You have 5 lives left
Type something: a
Word to guess: _____  You have 4 lives left
Type something: o
Word to guess: ____o_  You have 4 lives left
Type something: p
Word to guess: p___o_  You have 4 lives left
Type something: t
Word to guess: p_t_o_  You have 4 lives left
Type something: y
Word to guess: pyt_o_  You have 4 lives left
```

```
Type something: n
Word to guess: pyt_on You have 4 lives left
Type something: h
Well done, you got it!
```

We've written down our requirements in a very informal manner, along with some design notes, so we're now ready to start prototyping each part of the problem. It's here that the Python interactive prompt really shines as a means of trying out ideas before committing them to a full program. Let's look at each aspect in turn.

Prototyping a Solution

Selecting a Word

The first step in protyping this problem is to create a list of words. Next, we need to create a random index into that list.

Creating a Word List

The task of creating a word list is as simple as reading a file containing a list of words. We'll use a short text file for testing purposes. In the final version, something like a word-processor dictionary file would be a good source of words. Create a list of ten words in a file called words.txt, with one word per line. Now we can read that file into a list:

```
>>> wrdfile = open("words.txt","r")
>>> wordlist = wrdfile.readlines()
```

Generating a Random Index

To create a random index, we can use the random[1] function, which is found in the whrandom module. It will generate a fraction between 0 and 1. If we multiply this fraction by the length of the word list, we will almost have what we want. The problem is that we need an integer for the index but we have a fraction. Fortunately, Python provides the int() function, which rounds fractions down to the nearest integer value toward zero. Thus, to generate the index, we can try the following action:

```
>>> import whrandom
>>> index = int( whrandom.random() * len(wordlist) )
>>> print wordlist[index]
abacus
```

---

1. *Python actually has a* randint, *which does exactly what we want. The technique shown here, however, will work in nearly every language.*

Playing around with this code reveals a bug. If the random number is 1, then the index will be the length of the list. Because the list index starts at zero, we need to reduce the result by 1. Changing the index generation line to

```
>>> index = int( whrandom.random() * (len(wordlist) - 1) )
```

solves the problem. Now we can select a random word from the list!

Reading the Guesses

To read the guesses, we use our old friend `raw_input` and append the guess to a list of guesses:

```
>>> guesses = ""
>>> guess = raw_input("Next guess: ")
Next guess: a
>>> guesses = guesses + guess
```

That was easy. For the real game, we'll wrap the code in a loop that terminates when either the bad guess count reaches 6 or the word is guessed correctly, whichever comes first. We'll look at that issue later.

Keeping Score

Now we turn our attention to keeping track of the letters that have been guessed and the number of bad guesses. The second task is easy, because we need only an integer counter that goes from 0 to 6. The first task is more complex, and we have several options for handling it:

- A dictionary with each unique letter and a list of locations plus a flag to indicate whether it has been guessed

- A list of pairs containing the letter and the state

- A review of the previous guesses to see whether the letter has been guessed.

If we were dealing with a large quantity of text, we would probably use the first method because it is more efficient in terms of both storage and speed of lookup. The second technique is simple to implement and fairly fast. The last option is not very efficient if we were dealing with very long series of letters, but it is sufficient for our purposes as we have a maximum of 26 letters.[2] Let's try it out:

```
>>> target = wordlist[index] # should still be "abacus"
>>> guessed = 'aeiou'
```

---

2. Assuming we're using the English alphabet!

```
>>> displayword = ""
>>> for letter in target:
        if letter in guessed:
            displayword = displayword + letter
        else:
            displayword = displayword + "_"   .
```

```
>>> print displayword
a_a_u_
```

The final piece of the jigsaw is to identify whether the guess is valid and, if it is invalid to increment the bad_guess counter: The incrementation involves a straightforward if statement:

```
>>> if guess not in wordlist[index]:
        bad_guess = bad_guess + 1
```

Now that we have the separate bits of the program, let's try to stitch them together in a first attempt at a game of Hangman.

An Object Framework

We will build this application using objects. When we start to plan the classes needed in a particular program, we should think as abstractly as possible about what the program is actually doing. In our case, we are creating a *game* that comprises a number of *guesses* aimed at identifying some kind of *target* generated by the computer. The three nouns highlighted in that sentence form potential *candidate classes*. Let's look at each and see if we can define its *responsibilities*.

Game

The Game class will be the coordinating object responsible for displaying the game's status and directing the flow of events. It will also verify that the user is adhering to rules of the game.

Target

The Target class generates new targets for the player to guess. The appearance of a target will depend on the implementation. For example, in our Hangman game, the class will handle the reading of the word list and the generation of a random index. The Target class will also be responsible for comparing guesses with the target and returning an outcome.

Guess

The Guess class will have the job of combining one or more input mechanisms to generate the data needed to evaluate the outcome. The mechanism for capturing input and assembling it will obviously depend on the target, so the target and guess objects will be paired.

Outcome

In looking at these three classes, we have suggested the existence of an outcome. This outcome could be another class or perhaps a Boolean value indicating success. For the moment, we will defer a decision on this issue until we've seen how the pieces will fit together.

The Abstract Framework

Having thought about the design in terms of the required classes and their responsibilities, let's see if we can translate those ideas into Python code. First, we create the Game class:

```python
# Game looks after coordination and display
class Game:
    def __init__(self):
        self.theTarget = self.getTarget()
        self.GuessType = Guess          # see Note 1
        self.outcome = 1
        self.guesses = []


    # main function; checks score and stops when done
    def play(self):
        self.displayStart()
        while (self.outcome):
            self.guesses.append(self.GuessType())
            self.outcome = self.theTarget.eval(self.guesses[-1])
            self.display(self.outcome)


    # needs to be overridden to provide right kind of target
    def getTarget(self):
        return Target()
```

```
# play again; init values and redisplay first screen
def reStart(self):
    self.__init__()
    self.play()


# show opening screen; may have instructions, etc.
def displayStart(self):
    print """
Abstract class: Game.
You need to create an instance of some specific subclass!"""


# show appropriate display depending on outcome
def display(self, outcome):
    if outcome == 0:
        self.outcome = 0
```

■ *Note 1:* We created an attribute of Game called guessType to hold a reference to the type of guess we need to use. The play code is fairly generic except for the need to create the appropriate type of guess for our game. Because Python treats classes as objects, we can accomplish that task easily via the *class reference* guessType attribute, which can be altered by each subclass as necessary. This dynamic identification of type is easy in Python. In other object-oriented languages such as C++ or Java, where classes are treated as types but not as objects, you need to create a method that is overridden for each new game/guess type. I've illustrated this technique for the target that is generated by a getTarget method.

Next, we create a Guess class, which turns out to be pretty simple:

```
# get value(s) from user, present an object for evaluation
class Guess:
    def __init__(self):
        self.theValue = raw_input("Type something: ")


    def value(self):
        return self.theValue
```

Finally, we develop the Target class:

```
# Generate the object to be matched
# Check if a guess matches
class Target:
    def __init__(self):
        self.goal = self.getTarget()

    def getTarget(self):
        return 0

    def getGoal(self):
        return self.goal

    def eval(self, aGuess):
        return 0
```

Testing the Framework—A Simple Word Game

To see if our conceptual framework works, we need to try it out. The simplest game is one that picks a value (in this case, a name) from a list and asks the user to guess it. It reports the number of guesses required to get it right. To make the list of names available to both the Guess and Target classes, we could either make the names global or put them in the class. We don't want them to be part of the Game object, because the other classes would then be required to have a reference to the Game object, which is an unnecessary dependency. Instead, we create the names as a *class variable*—that is one shared by all instances of the NameGame class and accessed via the class itself. The code follows.

```
# simple guess-the-word game - precursor of Hangman!
class NameGame(Game):
    names = ['alan','fred','barney','heather','wilma','betty']
    def __init__(self):
        Game.__init__(self)
        self.failMsg = "Sorry, try again."
        self.successMsg = "Well done, you got %s after %d %s."
        self.guessString = 'guess'    # handle singular case
```

```
            self.theTarget = self.getTarget()
            self.GuessType = NameGuess    # change class reference
        def displayStart(self):
            print ("\n\n****************************")


        # override to provide NameTarget
        def getTarget(self):
            return NameTarget()


        def display(self,outcome):
            Game.display(self,outcome)
            if len(self.guesses) > 1:
                self.guessString = "guesses"
            if outcome:
                print self.failMsg
            else:
                print self.successMsg % (self.theTarget.getGoal(),
                                         len(self.guesses),
                                         self.guessString)
```

For the `Guess` class, we simply change the prompt to be more specific:

```
# display options and change default prompt
class NameGuess(Guess):
    def __init__(self):
        print NameGame.names
        self.theValue = raw_input("Type a name : ")
```

Finally, the `Target` class will simply select a name at random from the list stored in the `NameGame` class using the same random number technique we saw for choosing a word for Hangman.

```
# ask user for a word to guess; count number of guesses
# until right
class NameTarget(Target):
    def getTarget(self):
        import whrandom
        return NameGame.names[int( whrandom.random() * \
                         (len(NameGame.names) - 1) )]
```

```
def eval(self, aGuess):
    if self.goal == aGuess.value():
        return 0
    else:
        return 1
```

If you run this code, you should find that it works. Somehow, however, I don't think we've invented the next Quake just yet! Let's move on to our original objective of creating a game of Hangman.

Text-Based Hangman

We've figured out how to generate the target, and we know how to evaluate the guesses and how to read a guess. Now we want to use the `lives` feature to restrict the number of guesses. The display of the result is also more complex, because it must show the format of the target word, taking into account the guesses so far. As the display of the outcome is a responsibility of the `Game` object and the knowledge of the target is a responsibility of the `Target` object, we must cross the divide between these two objects.

In Python, we can access the `Goal` attribute of the `Target` from the `Game` object, because the `Game` has a reference to the `Target`. That approach, however, violates the principle of *information hiding*, whereby we try to prevent direct access to attributes and restrict clients of classes to calling methods only.[3] This technique has been found to make programs much easier to maintain in the long term, even if it does require a little bit of extra effort initially. To employ this technique, we create a `getGoal` method in the `Target` class that will return the current goal. The `Game` class will use this method and the list of guesses to generate the status display.

Notice, too, that we separate out the synthesis of the result string from the display method of the class. This division of duties will make life easier when we later create a GUI version of the game. Separating display tasks from computational tasks is usually a good idea, even if no immediate need to do so exists. You never know how other users of your classes might want to do things, so keep things as flexible as possible by making each method responsible for handling a specific set of tasks.

---

3. *If we were using a purist object-oriented environment such as Smalltalk, we couldn't access the* **Target** *'s goal attribute directly at all, because attributes are defined by the language as private—that is, they can be accessed only via methods.*

Let's create our Hangman Game class:

```
import game, whrandom, string, sys

########## GAME ##########
class Hangman(game.Game):
    wordfile = 'hangman.words'   # assume same folder
    def __init__(self):
        game.Game.__init__(self)
        self.guessType = hmGuess
        self.outcome = 6      # use outcome to count lives

    def displayStart(self):
        self.display(6)

    def getTarget(self):
        return hmTarget()

    def getResult(self):
        theWord = ''
        guessed = []
        # generate list of letters guessed so far
        if self.guesses:
            for g in self.guesses:
                guessed.append(g.value())
        # Now check target against guessed letters
        for c in self.theTarget.getGoal():
            if c in guessed:
                theWord = theWord + c
            else:
                theWord = theWord + "_"
        return theWord

    def display(self, outcome):
        theWord = self.getResult()
        # sort out plurals
```

```
            if  outcome == 1: lives = 'life'
             else: lives = 'lives'
            # check whether we got it right
            if '_' in theWord and  outcome == 0:
                print "Sorry you lose, the word was ", \
                        self.theTarget.getGoal()
             elif '_' not in theWord:
                print  "Well done, you got it!"
                sys.exit()
            else:
                print  "Word to guess: %s\t You have %d %s left" \
                        % (theWord, outcome, lives)
```

Notice that the `play` method is simply inherited from `Game`.

The `Guess` class has a bit extra work to do this time. It must validate the input, dealing with multiple letters and nonletters as appropriate:

```
########### GUESS ##########
class hmGuess(game.Guess):
    def __init__(self):
        self.theValue = raw_input("Next letter:   ")
        # check that the input is sensible
        if len(self.theValue) > 1:  # just use the first
            self.theValue = self.theValue[0]
        if self.theValue not in string.letters:
            self.theValue = raw_input("It must be a letter! ")


########## TARGET ##########
class hmTarget(game.Target):
    def __init__(self):
        self.lives = 6
        try:
            wrdFile = open(Hangman.wordfile, "r")
            wordList = wrdFile.readlines()
            wrdFile.close()
            index = int( whrandom.random() * (len(wordList)
                    - 1))
            self.goal = wordList[index][:-1] # lose \n
```

```
except IOError:
    print 'Failed to read file %s' % Hangman.wordfile
    sys.exit()

# eval returns the number of lives left
def eval(self, aGuess):
    if aGuess.value() not in self.goal:
        self.lives  = self.lives - 1
    return  self.lives
```

Let's create a GUI version of the Hangman game. We want such a version partly because it will look nicer and partly because doing so will introduce some interesting techniques and concepts that we haven't encountered before.

GUI Hangman

As we did with the grammar GUI, let's sketch the appearance of our GUI and identify the number of frames and components we will need. As shown in Figure 23-1, we will need two main frames: one for the display aspects and one for the controls at the bottom. The display frame will contain a graphic depicting the number of lives lost/remaining and a subframe containing the letters. The subframe consists of a number of rows, each of which will require a frame of its own. The control frame will display the word to be guessed and have **Reset** and **Quit** buttons.

Figure 23-1
Sketch of
proposed GUI
for Hangman
game

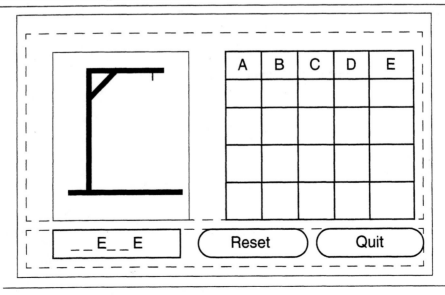

This setup is not unusual, and we've seen most of it before (apart from the graphic). Several specialized image modules are available for Tkinter that support sophisticated image types like JPEG and GIF. For our purposes, a Tkinter text widget will suffice because it can display simple embedded GIF files. We will need six versions of the diagram showing each of the six body stages required in Hangman. We can produce these images in any image editing program, including the Paint program that comes with Windows 98.

We can use Tkinter to construct this user interface:

```
####################
# GUI Hangman
#
# Author: A.J. Gauld
# Date:      15-04-2000
####################
from Tkinter import *
import hangman, string, sys

keys = [ ['A','B','C','D'],
         ['E','F','G','H'],
         ['I','J','K','L'],
         ['M','N','O','P'],
         ['Q','R','S','T'],
         ['U','V','W','X'],
            ['Y','Z'] ]
```

Here we import the modules needed and create a list of letters of the alphabet in the same layout that we will display them on the user interface. This technique of modeling the data to reflect how it will be used often makes life easier. We'll see how this particular layout works when we generate the letter keys. Note that instead of separating each individual letter, we could have used short strings: "ABCD", "EFGH", and so on. After all, Python treats strings as lists. The use of distinct letters is designed to make our intentions more obvious in this case.

Let's get the **Guess** class out of the way:

```
# same as previous guesses except it takes a value
# as an argument to the constructor
```

```
class hmGUIGuess( hangman.hmGuess ):
    def __init__(self, ch):
        self.theValue = string.lower(ch)
```

Now we write the Game class:

```
# Uses multiple inheritance. It is a type of Tkinter
# Frame object as well as a subclass of the Hangman
# game, so we inherit both.
class hmGUI(Frame, hangman.Hangman):
    def __init__(self,parent=0):
        self.imgpath = ''        # set if not same as program
        self.firstImg=self.imgpath+'hm6.gif'
        self.letters = {}
        hangman.Hangman.__init__(self)
        Frame.__init__(self,0)
        self.master.title("Hangman")
        self.displayStart ()
```

We use *multiple inheritance* for the hmGUI class because it is both an
instance of the Hangman game and a type of Tkinter Frame object. Multiple
inheritance works in the same way as the *single inheritance* that we've used
so far, except that Python will look for methods in *both* super classes. If a
method of the same name exists in both, then the first one found will be used.
Thus the order in which you list the superclasses can make a difference in
how your program behaves. Notice that our code explicitly calls both superclass constructors after doing the local initialization.

We continue with the Game subclass, looking at the other methods:

```
# For a GUI game the display function takes on a
# lot of responsibility for gluing the GUI to
# the underlying game objects
def display(self, chr):
    lossmsg = 'You lost! The word was\n\t%s'
    playmsg = 'Your target is:\n\t %s'
    successmsg = 'Well done, you guessed it!'

    # mark letter as used
    self.letters[chr].config(state=DISABLED)
```

```
# create a guess
self.guesses.append(hmGUIGuess(chr))


# decrease lives if wrong
self.outcome = self.theTarget.eval(self.guesses[-1])
if self.outcome > 0:        # we're still playing
    if '_' not in txt:  # and we've got it!
        txt = successmsg
    else: txt = playmsg % self.getResult()
else:
    txt = lossmsg % self.theTarget.getGoal()
self.status.configure(text=txt)


# update image
thefile = self.imgpath + 'hm' + str(self.outcome)\
            + '.gif'
self.theImg.configure(file=thefile)
```

To update the image on screen, we don't need to create a new image object. Instead, we simply change the file to which it refers. The text object contains the image object, which contains a file. The text object doesn't care about what the image object is displaying, just that we have an image to be displayed. It therefore delegates the responsibility for the display to the image object. This case is a fine example of the power of good object-oriented design.

```
def getTarget(self):
    return hangman.hmTarget()


def play(self):
    self.mainloop()


def quit(self):
    sys.exit()


def reset(self):
    # mark all letters unused
    for l in string.uppercase:
        self.letters[l].config(state=ACTIVE)
```

```
# reset the lives and guesses; create a new target
self.outcome = 6
self.guesses = []
self.theTarget = self.getTarget()

# reset the image and status
self.theImg.configure(file=self.firstImg)
txt = "Your target is:\n\t%s" % self.getResult()
self.status.configure(text=txt)
```

The latter two methods are the event handlers for the control buttons. The first is trivial; the second is of interest only because it creates a new hmTarget object, which ensures that we don't keep trying to guess the same word after a reset.

Now we build the GUI itself, which is the function of our displayStart method:

```
def displayStart(self):
    # create display frame with picture on left,
    # letters on right; picture goes inside a Text widget
    d = Frame(self)
    hm = Text(d, relief=SOLID, width=25, height=15)
    # create image object
    self.theImg = PhotoImage(file=self.firstImg)
    # insert @ line 1, char 0
    hm.image_create('1.0', image=self.theImg)
    hm.pack(side=LEFT, padx=20)
    # build the letter grid (see notes in book)
    ltr = Frame(d, border=1, relief=SUNKEN)
    for row in keys:
        f = Frame(ltr)
        for ch in row:
            action = lambda x=ch, s=self: s.display(x)
            self.letters[ch] = Button(f, text=ch,
                                      width=2,
                                      command=action)
```

```
                self.letters[ch].pack(side=LEFT)
        f.pack(pady=1)
    ltr.pack(side=LEFT)
    d.pack()


    # create control frame with status display left,
    # Reset button middle, and Quit button right
    c = Frame(self, border=1, relief=RAISED,
              background='blue')


    txt = "Your target is:\n\t%s" % self.getResult()
    self.status = Label(c, anchor=W,
                        background='blue', foreground='yellow',
                        width=25, text=txt)
    self.status.pack(side=LEFT,  anchor=W)


    r = Button(c, text='Reset', padx=10, command=self.reset)
    r.pack(side=LEFT, padx=10, pady=5, anchor=W)


    q = Button(c, text='Quit', padx=10, command=self.quit)
    q.pack(side=RIGHT, padx=20, pady=5, anchor=W)


    c.pack()
    self.pack()
```

Building the widgets follows the same mechanism as before, albeit with a few new configuration options. You will find these options explained in the online Tkinter tutorial. One part of the process loop deserves further explanation: the loop where we create the letter keys. This loop iterates over the list of keys we created at the beginning of the program and assigns a command action to each key. We could have created lots of individual methods, one per key, but instead we have used a feature called a *lambda function*. A lambda function is simply a function without a name. For example,

```
    spam = lambda: s = self, c = ch: s.display(c)
```

is exactly equivalent to

```
    def spam(s=self, c=ch): s.display(c)
```

We would have had to create 26 of these methods, one for each letter, each with its own default character. In contrast, using the lambda technique allows us to assign the default ch as part of the loop. It's also much less repetitive typing and, being a programmer, I'm lazy![4]

We start our game running by calling the play method on an instance of the game:

```
if __name__ == '__main__':
    hmGUI().play()
```

The end result looks like Figure 23-2.

Figure 23-2
Running the
Hangman game
program

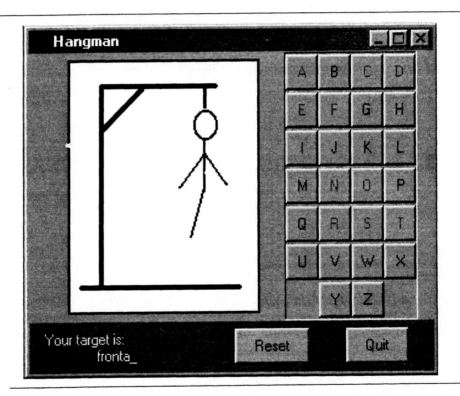

Other Ideas

Hangman is just one example of a guessing game that you could implement using this framework. The rest of this section lists other games that would work as well.

Mastermind

This game, which sometimes known as "bulls and cows," involves generating a target by picking four colors from a choice of six, with duplicates allowed. The player must then guess the colors and their order. The evaluation returns the number of colors in the right place (bulls) and the number of correct colors in the wrong place (cows). The player is restricted to a fixed number of guesses—usually six or ten. (It is important that a record of previous guesses be displayed to assist the player in working out his or her next guess.) The key feature from a programming perspective is the evaluation which must return two values—perhaps as a tuple?

Rock/Scissors/Paper

This well-known children's game involves the computer and player both generating "rock," "scissors," or "paper." Comparing the two values, rock breaks scissors, scissors cut paper, and paper wraps rock. In this way, a winner is calculated. The game consists either of a fixed number of guesses with the highest score winning or, alternatively, the first player to score some fixed number, five perhaps, winning. From a programming perspective, we need either to create a list of targets that we cycle through for each "guess" or to generate a new target for each "guess" submitted.

Things to Ponder

Can you think of other categories of games that might also share a common framework?

How could you extend this framework to cater for a more interactive style of game—for example, where a second player generates the target scenario rather than the computer?

Are there any restrictions on the types of games you could program in Python?

Minesweeper

This game is supplied with Microsoft Windows and has been cloned on virtually every platform. How the game is programmed will depend on how you represent the data. For example, you could use a table prepopulated with the display values (in which case, `eval` returns the contents of the selected square). Alternatively, you could calculate the value at the evaluation stage. The key programming feature in this game is the representation of the board. You will probably want to use a similar technique to the one used for the Hangman letter keys.

You can almost certainly think of other games that could use the framework developed in this chapter. Anything that involves the player guessing what the computer has decided should fit this pattern, and our framework will give you a starting point for a design. You can even invent your own games if you like.

Points to Remember

Object frameworks provide a way to reuse designs as well as code.

Frameworks are primarily concerned with defining an interobject messaging protocol.

Frameworks built on abstract classes generally provide substantial flexibility in the ways that you can use them. As a consequence, changes to your program over time are likely to be minimized.

Epilogue

We've come a long way since the start of the book. Ideally, you will have found it interesting and useful. I hope that I've inspired you to experiment further, using the information that you've gained here as a starting point to develop your own applications. When you feel confident with Python, look at some of the other languages mentioned in Appendix B. Certainly read some of the books described in Appendix C and check out the online resources as well.

In this book, you have learned not just how to program in Python, but how to program in general. That is, techniques are the same regardless of language. You should now feel confident in picking up even quite technical tutorials for other languages, because the jargon has been explained and you simply need to map the new material to what you already know. Programming is fundamentally concerned with breaking problems down into logical structures—either procedures and functions or, at a higher level of abstraction, into objects and modules. Most of all, you should embrace the challenges and try not to get too frustrated when things don't work out right the first time.

Appendices

This section is a potpourri of useful bits of information and pointers to other resources. It includes details about installing Python and IDLE, information about some other programming languages, a selection of references covering books and web pages.

Appendix

A Installing and Testing Python

These instructions are intended for Windows users. If you have Linux,[1] BeOS, or a Mac, then follow the instructions for your platform that are found on the Python Web site.

This appendix assumes that you have managed to get the Python installer, `py152.exe`, loaded onto your hard disk, either by downloading it from the Python Web site at

`http://www.python.org/download/download_windows.html`

or by copying the version on the CD-ROM. It assumes that you've copied the installer into the `C:\Temp` folder. If you put it somewhere else, substitute that folder for `C:\Temp` in the following instructions.

---

1. *Most Linux distributions have a version of Python available in a suitable package format such as Debian or Red Hat rpm. Check on your distribution CD. A Macintosh binary version is available on the Python site and other platforms are supported to varying degrees. Check out the Web site for the latest information.*

Running the Installer

From the Start | Run dialog, enter C:\Temp\py152.exe[2] and click OK. Select the default options by clicking Next or OK as requested by the wizard. After installing lots of files, the wizard will ask whether you want to install Tcl/Tk; respond Yes. The Tcl/Tk installer will start. Accept the default options until the installation process has completed.

You may be asked if you want to restart the system. If so, click OK. When Windows comes back, you will have Python installed on your system.

Testing the Installation

At the end of the installation, you should have an Explorer window showing the Tcl files. You might find it interesting to run the Widget Tour. If not, just close the window. Next, open Start | Programs | Python 1.5 | IDLE. A new window called Python Shell should appear with the Python interpreter prompt on display. (Figure A-1). If you got this far, then congratulations! Python is now correctly installed. You can now enter Python commands at that prompt or create, save, and run Python programs.

Figure A-1
Python Shell
window

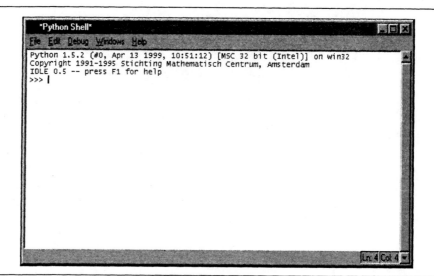

```
*Python Shell*                                                      _ □ ☒
File  Edit  Debug  Windows  Help
Python 1.5.2 (#0, Apr 13 1999, 10:51:12) [MSC 32 bit (Intel)] on win32
Copyright 1991-1995 Stichting Mathematisch Centrum, Amsterdam
IDLE 0.5 -- press F1 for help
>>> |
                                                                   Ln 4 Col 4
```

---

2. *If you downloaded the latest version from the Web site, then the installer file may have a different name.*

Running IDLE

IDLE is an *I*ntegrated *DeveL*opment *E*nvironment[3] for Python written in Python. It is somewhat experimental and does not offer the same level of help documentation as the other parts of the Python system. The good news is that it is fairly intuitive to use.

Using the Python Prompt

Start IDLE as described previously. You will be presented with a window containing the Python prompt. You can type commands there almost as you would with an MS-DOS version of Python. IDLE does, however, have a couple of differences that are designed to make life easier. First, IDLE will automatically indent your code where necessary. Second, the commands will be colored to reflect the syntax. A further advantage for Windows 95/98 users is that if you make a mistake, you can simply cursor up to the bad line and type `enter`. A copy of the line will be placed at the prompt, ready for you to edit to fix the error.[4] The program will still be lost when you exit IDLE, but you can save the session. Then using Notepad or some other text editor, you could edit out everything but the valid commands and create a program from a session file. There's also a better option, as we will see next.

Creating, Saving, and Running Programs from Files

Create a new window using `File|New Window` and type a Python program into the window that appears. Save the file with an extension of `.py` using `File|Save As`. You can now run that file by using `Edit|Run` (or by pressing the `F5` key[5]). An execution window will pop up displaying your output. If you need to modify your program, change back to the edit window and make the necessary corrections. Don't forget to close the output windows when you're finished with them or you will very soon have a large number cluttering up the screen.[6]

∎ *Note:* A new version of IDLE (version 0.5) was released while this book was being written. It is not included in the standard Python version 1.5.2 distribution but is well worth downloading. It offers significant improvements in the IDLE environment. To install it, simply unzip the files under the `Python\Tools` folder and edit the IDLE shortcut to point to the new version

---

3. Officially, it stands for Integrated DeveLopment Environment, but given Python's traditional links with the Monty Python TV series, it may also be named after one of the stars: Eric Idle. What do you think?
4. NT users have the ability within a Command Prompt window to recall previous commands, so this feature is less of an advantage for them.
5. In the latest version of IDLE, this shortcut is `Ctrl-F5`.
6. The new version of IDLE uses the Python Shell window for output so you no longer have the problem of too many windows being open.

of `idle.pyc`. IDLE is very much a moving target, and it's a good idea to keep an eye on the current state of play. The latest news is to be found on the Python web site in the area dedicated to IDLE.

A Final Touch

It's a good idea to create a folder for your Python project files. This folder should be set in an environment variable called PYTHONPATH, which, unfortunately the installer does not create for you. You set it by opening `C:\AUTOEXEC.BAT` in Notepad and adding the line

```
SET PYTHONPATH=C:\Projects
```

where `C:\Projects` is whatever you called your new folder.

You can add other directories using the same syntax as the MS-DOS PATH environment variable.

The next time you start your PC and run a Python program, Python will know to look for your files in that directory if you try to `import` them or issue an `import` command at the Python prompt.

Appendix
B Some Interesting Programming Languages

This appendix describes some popular—and some less popular but nonetheless interesting—programming languages for you to investigate should you grow bored with Python. Programmers should generally learn several languages, because understanding the unique features of one language can help you see different ways of using other languages. For example, people who have never used a language that provides a dictionary type often cannot appreciate how much easier life can become with such a construct.

Each description provides some background information about that language's history and areas of use. It also includes a simple "Hello world" program that illustrates how to define a class with methods, conditional statements, and looping constructs and how to instantiate a class and send a message to the resultant object. We conclude with some information about availability of free or evaluation copies of the software necessary to use the language.

Python

We'll start with Python because by now it should be a known reference point. Python was invented by Guido Van Rossum and is named after the BBC comedy show "Monty Python's Flying Circus." It is a very simple language with many powerful features. It supports several styles of programming, including object-oriented programming and functional programming as well as traditional imperative or procedural styles.

Python comes with a large library of modules, and many more are available for downloading. Python is suitable for a wide range of tasks. Only very technical, low-level programming tasks or those requiring very high execution speeds are really outside its scope.

Hello World

The Python version of "Hello world" follows:

```
class Message:
    def __init__(self, s=''):
        self.txt = s


    def printIt():
        if self.txt == '':
            print 'No message'
        else:
            for i in range(3):
                print self.txt


m = Message('Hello world')
m.printIt()
```

Availability

See the main text and Appendix A for details on how to obtain and install Python.

BASIC

BASIC stands for Beginner's All-purpose Symbolic Instruction Code. As its name suggests, this language was one of the earliest attempts to produce a beginner's programming language. Designed in the 1960s, early BASIC was very limited, relying on numbered lines and GOTO statements to control the program while variables were restricted to single letters. Over time BASIC has evolved substantially. Arguably the best version currently available is Microsoft's Visual Basic for Applications (VBA or just plain VB). A cut-down version of VB called VBScript exists, and an interpreter for it is installed by default in recent versions of Windows.

VB provides most of the features of a modern programming language, including classes and objects. It is undoubtedly the easiest way to access Microsoft's COM objects, which form the foundation of Microsoft's operating systems and applications. Much unjustified derision has been aimed at VB. It does have limitations, but it also does its intended job very well.

Hello World

A VBScript "Hello world" follows:

```
class Message
    Private theTxt
    Public Property Let Txt(S)
        theTxt = S
    End Property
    Public Sub Print()
        If theTxt = "" Then
            WScript.echo "No message"
        Else
            For i = 1 to 3
                WScript.echo theTxt
            Next
        End If
    End Sub
End Class
```

```
Dim M
set M = new Message
M.txt = "Hello world"
m.Print( )
```

Availability

Whereas VB is a commercial product, VBScript is freely available on Windows platforms, either preinstalled with Windows 98 or Internet Explorer 5 or by downloading from Microsoft's MSDN Web site. Commercial versions of VB are available for most development needs, from the home user to the professional corporate programmer.

Other Versions of BASIC

Other versions of BASIC are also available, including more traditional derivatives of the original. Some of these versions target specific programming niches, such as controlling industrial machinery or data-logging devices. Others follow in the original tradition of BASIC as a command-line, interpreted, general-purpose language. In addition, several clones of VB provide macro or extension languages to applications as diverse as project management tools and terminal emulators. There are even commercial VB clones available for UNIX that provide for complete portability between Windows and UNIX versions of applications.

C/C++

C++ is a superset of C[1] that adds object-orientation features. Both languages are heavily used in the software industry for creating commercial applications and for large projects. They provide features for accessing hardware as well as the operating system at a very low level. In addition, both compile to native code. With suitable optimization the resultant programs can be very fast, often comparable to assembler. The downside of this power is that both languages—but especially C++—are complicated to learn and use, requiring great skill on the part of the programmer. It is possible to produce clear, easy-to-read code in C++ but you have to work at it.

---

1. *Minor inconsistencies do exist between the languages. Also C++ adds several useful non-object-oriented features to C, earning C++ the description of being "a better C." Experienced C programmers often disagree with that description!*

Hello World

The "Hello World" program looks like this in C++:

```
#include <iostream.h>
#include <string.h>

class Message{
private: char txt[50];
public:
    Message(char* s){ strcpy(txt,s);};
    void print();
};

void Message::print()
{
    if (!strcmp(txt,""))
        cout << "No message";
    else for (int i = 0; i< 3; i++)
        cout << txt << "\n";
}

int main()
{   Message m("Hello world");
    m.print();
    return 0;
}
```

Availability

The GNU Option
GNU has produced a very good compiler for both C and C++ that is available for free for many platforms. It is command-line-based, but development environments are available to simplify its use.

The Borland Alternative
During the writing of this book, Borland released its C/C++ compiler as a free download. It is only the command-line version but represents a full implementation of the commercial product used as the engine behind Borland's commercial development tools.

Java

Java is one of the hot topics of modern programming. It has its roots as a small language for embedded systems, but arrived almost at the same time as the World Wide Web. Its potential for downloading applets and other Web-compatible features was soon spotted. This object-oriented language shares many similarities to Python but uses a two-stage compile/run strategy. It does not compile to native code[2] but rather to a portable byte code format (somewhat like Python .pyc files), which is then run within the Java Virtual Machine (JVM). The JVM has been ported to many computer architectures and gives Java its much-vaunted portability. In fact, there is nothing much new in this approach; similar techniques have been around for at least 25 years.

Java's syntax is derived from C and thus is superficially similar to C, C++, Perl, Tcl, JavaScript, and several other languages. Java has some odd inconsistencies in its language definition, which detract from its ease of learning. Nevertheless, this language is still much easier to learn than C++. Java also comes with a large number of classes for doing string manipulation, network programming, and other tasks.

Hello World
A simple "Hello World" program in Java follows:

```
class Msg{
    private String txt;
    public Msg(String s){
        txt = s;
    }
    public void print(){
        if (txt == "")
            System.out.println("No message");
```

---

2. *Native code compilers are becoming available but they are not currently the norm within the Java community. Indeed, some Java programmers actively dislike them, seeing them as a threat to Java's promise of portability.*

```
              else
                 for(int i = 0;i<3;i++)
                      System.out.println(txt);
              }
       }


       public class test{
           public static void main(String args[]){
              Msg m = new Msg("hello world");
              m.print();
              }
       }
```

Availability

The Java Development Kit (JDK) is available as a free download from Sun. It provides the basic command-line tools—compiler, debugger, JVM, and so on—needed to create and run Java programs, along with the large standard class library. Various commercial tools are also available for Java development, including such extras as GUI building tools.

Object Pascal (Delphi)

Pascal was invented by Nicklaus Wirth as a teaching language. It was named after the mathematician Blaise Pascal. The original Pascal was so focused on teaching good programming habits that it punished any carelessness in type consistency or syntax and thus became known as a very unforgiving language. Later industrial versions of Pascal were less strict and introduced such features as string types that were absent from the original. Eventually, object orientation features appeared, and the resulting Object Pascal was used to create the early Apple Macintosh applications. Borland had been at the forefront of the push to have Pascal adopted as a commercial language and its Turbo Pascal product quickly adopted the object orientation extensions. This version gradually evolved into the Delphi development tool, which uses Object Pascal as its programming language.

Hello World

A Delphi "Hello world" program follows:

```
program Hello;
{$APPTYPE CONSOLE}

type
    Message = class
    txt : string;
    constructor create(s:string);
    procedure print;
end;

constructor Message.Create(s:string);
begin
    txt := s
end;

procedure Message.print;
var i : integer;
begin
    if txt = '' then
        writeln ('No message')
    else
        for i := 1 to 3 do
            writeln(txt);
end;

var m : Message;
begin
    m := Message.Create('Hello world');
    m.print();
end.
```

Availability

Delphi comes with an extensive class library and some very good tools. It is not free, however. A Free Pascal Compiler (FPC) provides very good compatibility with Delphi's Object Pascal language but lacks the extensive class library. An open source project is under way to provide a similar development environment.

Perl

Perl was created by Larry Wall and stands for the Practical Extraction and Reporting Language, or, alternatively, the Pathetically Eclectic Rubbish Lister. This dual name feature is in keeping with Perl's underlying principle that "there's more than one way to do it." As a consequence, Perl nearly always provides several mechanisms to accomplish a task, such as many different loop and conditional constructs. This language was designed to provide the best facilities of the UNIX command shells plus the utility programs awk and sed. Until the creation of Perl, UNIX system administrators had to write utilities using a convoluted combination of shell programs combined with sed or awk programs. Perl allowed the same utilities to be written in a single file using a single language—usually running faster, too. It caught on in a big way and is now available on many platforms. Perl does much more than simple text processing. If Python has a natural competitor in the programming world, Perl is it.

Perl provides all of the features of Python, often with an increase in running speed. The downside is that the syntax of Perl is more cumbersome and the resultant code can be extremely difficult to read. Perl's object orientation features are less well integrated than those in Python. On the other hand, Perl provides very fast, very powerful, built-in regular expression capability.

Perl has established itself as the de facto standard for CGI[3] programming on the World Wide Web.

---

3. *CGI—the Common Gateway Interface—is the most common mechanism used today for Web servers to provide dynamic content such as search engines and Web counters.*

Hello World

A Perl "Hello world" program requires us to put the class in a separate module file with the same name as the class and then call that file from the program. First, we create the module, Message.pm:

```perl
package Message;
# Message class constructor
sub new {
    my $class = shift;
    my $self = {};
    $self->{txt} = shift;
    bless ($self, $class);
    return $self;
}
# Method definition
sub print{
    if $self->{txt} eq "" {
        print "No message";
    }else{
        for ($i = 0; $i < 3; $i++){
            print $self->{txt},"\n"
        }
    }
}
1; # perl packages must return "true"!
```

In the program file, hello.pl, we add the following code:

```perl
use Message;

$m = Message->new("Hello World");
$m->print()
```

Availability

Perl is available for many platforms. The best place to look for Perl information is:

```
http://www.perl.com/perl/
```

There are many books available on Perl from many authors and publishers. Pick your favorite.

Smalltalk

Smalltalk is the grandaddy of object-oriented programming. Although other languages[4] were doing object-oriented things before Xerox Parc released Smalltalk 80, it was Smalltalk 80 that really caught the programming public's attention. In Smalltalk, absolutely everything is an object. That setup makes the syntax very consistent, although not quite as easy to learn as some of its proponents would suggest. It does have a huge class library and a very good development environment. Smalltalk encourages an exploratory style of development not unlike that used in Python when experimenting with the Python interactive prompt.

Hello World

A Smalltalk "Hello world" program separates class definition from the program:

```
Object subclass: #Msg
    InstanceVariableNames 'txt'
withText: aString
    txt := aString
printOn: aStream
    (txt class = UndefinedObject)
        ifTrue: [ aStream nextPutAll: 'No message']
        ifFalse: [ 3 timesRepeat: [aStream nextPutAll: txt]]
```

---

4. *Simula added object orientation features to Algol in the 1960s, and several dialects of Lisp had object orientation capabilities added throughout the 1970s and 1980s.*

Now we have to create an instance and print the message using the inherited `printString` method, which calls the `printOn` method we defined using the console "stream":

```
m := Msg withText: 'Hello world'
m printString
```

Availability

A number of free Smalltalk versions are available. Perhaps the most interesting is Squeak, which provides insight into the original Parc Place Smalltalk 80, including its GUI. This version was similar to the GUI that inspired Steve Jobs to build the Macintosh. Squeak was developed by Apple's research team as described in the following quote from the Web site:

> *Squeak began, very simply, with the needs of a research group at Apple. We wanted a system as expressive and immediate as Smalltalk to pursue various application goals (prototypical educational software, user interface experiments and (let's be honest) another run at the Dynabook fence.*

For building production-quality Smalltalk programs for Windows, you can try Dolphin Smalltalk by Object Arts, which produces a free, albeit slightly crippled evaluation version (with superb documentation) as well as a full commercial product.

Interesting Alternatives

Several languages are mentioned briefly in this section, just to alert you to their existence. Each has special features of interest and, for one reason or another, does not follow the mainstream in the way it works. Consequently, you'll need to put out a bit more effort to learn these languages, but the effort will reward you with a new insight into how programs and computers work.

Awk

Awk stands for Aho, Weinberger, Kernighan—the surnames of the three authors of the language. Awk fills a very specialized niche and does so spectacularly well. It works by matching code blocks to regular expressions. That is, whenever a line of input matches any of the regular expressions, the corresponding code blocks are executed. In Python terms, this operation is equivalent to the following code:

```
import re
f = open('somefile.txt','r')
```

```
for line in f.readlines():
    if re.search(RE1, line): FUN1(line)
    if re.search(RE2, line): FUN2(line)
    # etc. for an arbitrary number of REs
f.close()
```

In contrast, awk automatically opens the file, reads it, checks the regular expressions, and then splits the line into fields for you, which makes writing programs that analyze files line by line very easy.

Eiffel

Eiffel is a programming language designed by Bertrand Meyer and described in his book *Object Oriented Software Construction*. In many ways, it is an idealized language incorporating Meyer's ideas on how large software systems should be built. A great deal of emphasis is placed on designing clear interfaces between components. Many object orientation practitioners (including me) think that Eiffel deserves a much wider audience, but the marketplace in general does not agree!

Lisp

Lisp (List Processing) is another very old computer language; it was invented by John McArthy in the early 1960s. It is still very popular both as a language for programming artificial intelligence applications and research and as an embedded macro language. Lisp is an incredibly simple language syntactically but has very powerful capabilities. Common Lisp and its object-oriented add-on, CLOS, are extremely powerful programming tools that take a long time to learn fully but can be used by a beginner with very little instruction.

Scheme is a slightly more conventional language that is heavily based on Lisp. Several free versions of Scheme are available for the curious. The Emacs editor also comes with its own variant of Lisp, which is perfectly adequate for introductory experimentation.

Prolog

Prolog (Programming Logic) is a direct competitor to Lisp in the artificial intelligence arena. It is fundamentally different in approach to any of the other languages described in this appendix. Essentially, a Prolog program is a description of the problem; Prolog uses a built-in rules engine to derive a solution to this problem. Prolog is the only language mentioned here whose control constructs do not map easily onto the things you've learned about in Python. Prolog is worth checking out just because it is so different.

Ruby

Ruby is the new kid on the block. It tries to combine the elegance of Python and the raw power of Perl. At the time of writing, few books on Ruby had been published, although that situation should change soon. Ruby is growing in power and support and, because of its similarities to Python, might be worth a look.

Tcl/Tk

The Tool Control Language (Tcl) and its associated GUI Toolkit (Tk) were invented by John Ousterhout as a language for embedding in applications. Tcl has some unusual features that make it worthy of study. In particular, every aspect of the language is defined as a function (in Tcl speak, a "command"). Thus a while loop is a command with two parameters: a Boolean test and a block of code. Consequently, the programmer can redefine the behavior of any aspect of the language and invent not just new functions, but also new control structures.

Tk is the underlying GUI widget set for Python's Tkinter. It has also been used as the basis for Perl's GUI tools.

Appendix
C
Resources

Books to Read

Python

Learning Python
Mark Lutz, David Ascher, Frank Wilson; O'Reilly; 1999

Probably the best book on starting to program in Python if you already know another language. Typical O'Reilly style. If you don't like that you may prefer some others mentioned here.

Internet Programming with Python
Aaron Waters, Guido van Rossum, James Ahlstrom; IDG Books; 1996

Written by, among others, the language's creator with a strong bias to Internet programming including HTML, CGI, and general sockets. It has a good language tutorial at the beginning.

Programming Python
Mark Lutz; O'Reilly; 1996

The classic text. It describes the whys and wherefores of the language better than the other books, and it is strong on modules and object-oriented programming. It also gives an intro to Tkinter programming. It is becoming a bit dated now, although the core language features are still the same.

Python and Tkinter Programming
John Grayson; Manning; 1999

At the time of writing the only book on Tkinter programming. Lots of reference material and some fairly complex projects. Does rely heavily on the PMW widget set, which doesn't come standard with Python.

Mastering Regular Expressions
J. E. F. Friedl; O'Reilly; 1997

The definitive book on Perl regular expressions. Python does not follow Perl's rules exactly, but this text is still the best general guide to using regular expressions available.

Tcl/Tk in a Nutshell
Paul Raines, Jeff Tranter; O'Reilly; 1999

Because of the dearth of books on Tkinter, this text tends to be my first port of call when looking for information on Tk widgets. You have to convert from the original Tcl style to Tkinter's object-oriented format, but once you get used to it that's pretty easy. You can also use it to learn Tcl/Tk, which is an interesting language in its own right and comes for free with Python. Why not give it a whirl?

Other Languages

C/C++
Many books focus on C/C++. The only two that I recommend have been around for a long time and are tried and proven.

The C Programming Language, Second Edition
Brian Kernighan, Dennis Ritchie; Prentice Hall; 1988

Very complete and surprisingly short description of the original C language. One of the best language references ever written.

C++ Primer, Third Edition
Stanley Lippman, Josée Lajoie; Addison-Wesley; 1998

A good overview of C++ covering the base language. The latest version includes the features incorporated into the ANSI/ISO standard.

Java
I've yet to find a really good book on Java. The best I can recommend is that you browse your local bookshop or online store and see what appeals to your taste and pocketbook.

BASIC
Many books on BASIC exist, covering each of its many dialects. If you are serious about pursuing programming in BASIC, especially on the PC, then I strongly recommend using Visual Basic and studying any of the many books on that version. A good introduction for zero cost is to use VBScript within WSH. I have found the following tutorial on WSH especially useful:

Windows Script Host—A Programmers Reference
Dino Esposito; Wrox Press; 1999

Does a good job of explaining the WSH object model and contains some very brief reference material on VBScript. Combined with the online help files for WSH, you can just about learn VBScript this way.

Delphi/Object Pascal
Lots of Delphi books are available. I have found several that I like. If I had to select only one it would be the following:

Mastering Delphi 5
Marco Cantu; Sybex International; 1999

The latest in a long series going back to the original release of Delphi. The style is easy to follow, and the code segments are very well thought out and illustrate the points concisely.

Perl
Learning Perl, Second Edition
Randal Schwartz, Tom Christiansen; O'Reilly; 1997

The standard introductory text. Doesn't cover all of the features of Perl but does get the main points across in an easy-to-follow manner.

Smalltalk
Once again I can't recommend a book on Smalltalk. I have found the best introduction to be the online tutorial at the Object Arts Web site.

General Programming
There are some classic programming texts that any serious programmer should own and read regularly. Here are my personal favorites:

Code Complete
Steve McConnell; Microsoft Press; 1993

The most complete reference on all things to do with writing code that I know. I read it after several years of experience and it all rang true—I even learned some new tricks. It literally changed the way I wrote programs. Buy it—now!

Programming Pearls
Jon Bentley; Addison-Wesley; 1986,1989,1999

There are two volumes, both invaluable. Bentley shows how to improve the efficiency of your programs in every conceivable way, from concept through design to implementation.

These books are part of a programming library that came out of Bell Labs in the 1980s in the wake of UNIX. There are so many classics in this series that I will simply say that anything from the pens of Ken Thompson, Jon Bentley, Dennis Ritchie, Andrew Keonig, and the rest of the gang at Bell Labs is worth reading. The styles may vary but the content is pure gold.

The Pragmatic Programmer
Andrew Hunt, David Thomas; Addison-Wesley; 2000

This text is almost a sequel to the book you hold in your hands, in that it looks at the working practices and techniques needed to move up a rung from beginner to professional programmer. The book is crammed with hints and tips that are normally learned the hard way. Reading this book could save you some pain.

The Art of Computer Programming (Box Set)
Donald Knuth; Addison-Wesley; 1999

This set of three books describes fundamental algorithms that are used by programmers over and over again. It's heavy-going and a bit mathematical, but if you are concerned about the efficiency and absolute correctness of your programs, these texts are worth searching out. The entire set has recently been reissued with some updates.

Object-Oriented Programming

I've already mentioned these, but here they are again anyway.

Object-Oriented Analysis
Peter Coad, Ed Yourdon; Yourdon Press; 1991

A great intro to object-oriented concepts with a very simple notation for re-cording your designs. As an added bonus, the notation is very similar to the new Unified Modeling Language (UML) standard that is being adopted by most books, tools, and journals. There are follow-up books on design and programming but the analysis text is the best of the three.

Object-Oriented Analysis and Design with Applications
Grady Booch; Benjamin Cummings; 1994

Another excellent book, moving more into the detail of designing classes and objects. The first edition, if you can find it, illustrates the lessons in five differ-ent object-orientation languages. The second edition uses only C++ and is the poorer for it. The book uses Booch's own notation, which is still the best notation around, though is being eclipsed by UML and so is effectively obso-lete. Booch is reputed to be bringing out a new edition using UML, but it's been a long time coming.

Object-Oriented Software Construction, Second Edition
Bertrand Meyer; Prentice Hall; 2000

Meyer has his own object-oriented programming language—Eiffel—and uses it to teach object-orientation very effectively. Because Eiffel is (unfairly) a bit of a minority interest, the book takes a little extra effort to read. It is undoubt-edly worth it for the sheer breadth of coverage of the current object-oriented technology scene.

Other books worth reading include the following:

Design Patterns: Elements of Reusable Object-Oriented Software
Erich Gamma, et al.; Addison-Wesley; 1995

A revolutionary book when it came out. It contains a number of common object-oriented design patterns and, perhaps more importantly, a notation for documenting them. There is now a flourishing patterns discussion and a dedicated Web site with many additional patterns as well as variations of the ones in the book.

"Clouds to Code"
Jesse Liberty; Wrox Press; 1997

This book takes you through the process of building a real object-oriented application—warts and all. It's rather like our case studies but much bigger and includes use of design tools like UML.

UML Distilled, Second Edition
Martin Fowler, Kendall Scott; Addison-Wesley; 2000

A very brief but practical guide to UML. It demonstrates all stages of the design process and explains how UML can be applied.

Web Sites to Visit

Languages

Python
The Python Web site:

```
http://www.python.org/
```

Mark Hammond's Python Starship connecting Microsoft Windows and Python:

```
http://starship.python.net/crew/mhammond/
```

A Web server development environment using Python:

```
http://www.zope.org/
```

Tcl/Tk
The home of Tcl and Tk information (and by implication useful Tkinter information), (at the time of writing):

```
http://dev.scriptics.com/
```

The host company Scriptics has recently changed its name to Ajuba, however, so the site may follow suit.

BASIC
The Microsoft Web site for Visual Basic info:

```
http://msdn.microsoft.com/vbasic/
```

Glossary

This glossary is not intended to be a complete dictionary of computing. Neither does it define every term used in this book. Instead, it expands on terms that are described only in passing or are referenced without explanation. In general, if you find a term in the book without explanation that you don't understand, then there's a good chance you'll find some more information here.

Abstract Class: A class that is not intended to be used for creating *instances* but rather provides an *interface* that is implemented by derived classes. Some languages offer syntactic support for abstract classes, in Python, it is up to the programmer to respect the intent.

ActiveX Object: *See COM Object.*

API: *Application Programmers Interface.* A defined set of functions that a programmer can call to perform tasks. The operating system usually provides an API to access the computer's hardware. This API will be implemented by each hardware supplier so that regardless of the make of, for example, the video card installed, the programmer can write a single set of function calls to draw a square or circle (or perform any other task). Similarly, a module such as Python's sys module provides an API for such things as exiting from Python.

Argument: The value passed to a function. The corresponding *parameter* in the function definition takes on the value of the argument for the duration of the function call. If the argument is a reference to a variable, then the function may be able to change the value of the variable.

ASCII: *American Standard Code for Information Interchange.* The traditional encoding of the set of characters used by computers into numbers. This code specifies 7 bits and therefore encodes 128 different characters. This number has proved insufficient for multilingual use, and newer character codings exist. ASCII is still widely used, however, because it is simple to work with and understand.

Assembler: An early attempt to make computer programming easier for humans. It simply created short acronyms for each of the numeric codes used by the computer *processor* to represent instructions. Typical acronyms were: ADD, SUB, MOVE, and JMP.

Attribute: A field within a class. It can be used to refer to data fields or methods but most commonly refers to data fields.

Binary: The name of the base-2 number system. In base 2, each digit can be represented by either 0 or 1; these digits, in turn, can be represented by switches in a *processor* that are on or off or by the north/south polarities of magnetic fields. This simple concept is the basis of digital computing. Binary has since come to mean any form of pure data represented as binary digits. The decimal number 12 is represented as 1100 in binary.

Bit: *Binary digit.* The basic unit of the *binary* system. A bit can take the value 1 or 0.

Black Box: A term that comes from traditional engineering. It refers to any component that has a set of inputs and a set of outputs that can be used for some purpose without the user needing to know what happens inside the box. Thus, when we buy a new TV, we know that we must plug in an antenna or other source of video signal and that we must switch it on and select channels. On the other hand, we don't need to know how the TV works internally. In programming, the functions provided in the *standard library* work in the same way. That is, we use them without needing to know how they work; we just accept that they will.

Block: A sequence of one or more code statements executed within a single logical programming construct. A block can include other blocks. In an `if/elif/else` or `case` construct, a block of code will exist for each of the conditional statements.

Byte: Eight *bits*; sometimes—usually in the context of protocol descriptions—called an octet.

Catch: The act of handling an error *raised* elsewhere in a program or by the *standard library*. Catch is applied only to the `try/except` style of error handling. *See also Exception Handler.*

Class: A description of a set of *objects*. A class describes the *attributes* and *methods* common to all objects in the set. Classes can inherit capabilities from other classes.

Code: In the context of an ASCII string of characters, the number used to represent the ASCII character. Within the context of programming, the code is shorthand for *source code*.

COM: Component Object Model. Microsoft's specification for a mechanism that allows software components to be built in any programming language and used in any programming language. In practice, the technique is used only on Microsoft's own *platforms*. An extension to COM known as Distributed COM (DCOM) allows the components to be used even when they reside on another computer. Competing technologies include the Common Object Request Broker Architecture (CORBA) and Enterprise JavaBeans (EJB).

COM Object: A component that meets the *COM* specification.

Command Prompt: A prompt at which commands are typed. In the context of this book, it is either the operating system prompt (C:> in MS-DOS) or the Python interactive prompt (>>>).

Compiler: A translator that converts *source code* into *object code*, usually saving the results to a file. The output file may be directly executable or it may require linkage with an operating environment before it will execute. In languages like Perl, Python, and Java, the compiler output takes on a more platform-independent format that requires an interpreter to perform a last stage of translation to native machine code. In practice, this approach has proved an effective way of achieving "fast enough" performance without sacrificing cross-platform portability.

Component: Another name for a programming *black box*. COM objects are examples of components.

Concatenation: The joining of two or more items (often strings) together.

Concrete Class: A class from which instances are expected to be created. The complement of an *abstract class*.

Constructor: A special method that runs when an instance of a class is created. It performs *initialization* for the new object. In Python, the constructor is the __init__() method.

Destructor: A special method that runs when an instance of a class is destroyed. It performs *finalization* for the object. In Python, the destructor is the (infrequently seen) __del__() method.

DOS: *Disk Operating System*. Microsoft's precursor to Windows. A DOS-compatible environment is available under Windows under the various names: DOS box, command prompt, MS-DOS prompt. They are all effectively the same; the result is either a window containing a DOS *command prompt* or a full-screen MS-DOS session.

DOS Prompt: *DOS* version of a *command prompt*.

Environment Variable: A special *variable* created and maintained within the operating system and made available to programs. Typically, it stores system-specific information. On Windows platforms, environment variables are gradually being replaced by *registry* entries.

EOF: *End of file* marker. Every operating system uses a special character to indicate the end of a file. For example, in DOS it is CTRL-Z; on UNIX it is CTRL-D. Most programming languages provide a function to allow you to test for EOF.

Error: A mistake! Usually the programming environment will detect errors and report them. Sometimes you will have made a typing mistake; at other times something will have happened that you did not expect and did not account for in your program. This latter category of error is often called an *exception*.

Exception: *See Error*.

Exception Handler: A piece of code that deals with errors *raised* elsewhere in the program or in the *standard library* functions. Usually these blocks are identified by the try/except syntax. Traditional if/else tests may also be referred to as exception or error handlers.

Executable: A file that can be executed. Users often refer to such a file as a *program*. Executables are generated by *compilers*.

Field: *See Attribute*.

Finalization: The code run at the end of a function, class, module, or program that cleans up any loose ends. In the absence of garbage collection, it will typically delete any variables created, close files that were opened, and so forth.

Floating Point: Numbers that can contain fractions, so called because the decimal point can appear anywhere in the number. For example, both 1.23456 and 1234.56 are floating-point numbers; they both contain a decimal point, albeit in different places. (Some programming languages provide fixed-point numbers, typically for storing monetary values.) The internal representation of these numbers uses an exponent system that describes the size of the numbers and thus allows them to store very large or very small values.

GUI: *Graphical User Interface.* The alternative to a command line. In this scenario, the features of the computer are represented by graphical icons and a pointing device is used to activate operations either via the icons or menu selections. This type of interface is also known as a WIMP (*Windows Icons Menus* and *Pointers*) interface.

High-Level Language: Programming languages have been categorized into different levels according to the amount of abstraction in the underlying computer architecture. Machine code is level 1, assembler is level 2, the languages we look at in this book are nearly all level 3,[1] and a few specialized reporting languages are described as level 4 (also known as 4GL, for fourth generation language). Much effort has been put into developing a fifth generation language, so far without much success—possibly because no one agrees on exactly what that really means!

Information Hiding: A concept akin to a *black box*. The idea is to conceal the implementation of an object or module from the user, presenting only a functional interface that he or she can use. This concept is sometimes referred to as encapsulation, although this term can also have the broader meaning of binding data and related functions together in a single module or object.

Initialization: The code that runs first in a function, object, module, or *program* and that creates the necessary resources and environment for the program to do its job. When dealing with objects, initialization is often carried out by a special *method* called a *constructor*.

Instance: A specific occurrence of a data type, taking up space in memory and usually referenced by a *variable*. When applied to classes and objects, it can be viewed as a synonym for *object*.

Integer: A whole number that may be either positive or negative. It is limited in range by the number of bits used by the computer to a value known as *MAXINT*. On a 32-bit computer this value is approximately +/- 2 billion.

---

1. *Prolog can be viewed as a fourth generation language. Some of its more vociferous proponents have even suggested that Prolog is a fifth generation language!*

Interface: The capabilities of a component, module, or other software artifact that are available to users of the artifact. In the context of objects, it usually refers to the set of methods exposed by a class.

Interpreter: Takes a file of source code and executes it. This stage may consist of a line-by-line translation, or it may involve compiling the source code into object code "on the fly" and then running the object code. The interpreter might store the object code as a file for future use. Python generates an object file on the first `import` operation. If the source file is older than the object file, it will use the latter on subsequent invocations.

Iteration: The execution of a *block* of code within a loop construct. The full execution of a loop will typically involve several iterations of the loop body.

Linux: An open source, free version of a UNIX-like operating system that has become very popular. Linux (like UNIX) is much more complex than pure GUI-based operating systems for a beginner to set up, although several groups are trying to address this issue. It is very stable and for programmers offers a huge quantity of programming languages and tools, nearly all free!

Long Integer: Notionally a long integer is just like a regular integer but with a larger limit on its size. In practice, its usage depends on a combination of the programming language and environment. In some implementations of C, there is no difference between the two integer types! In other languages, including Python, a long integer is one with no size limit. This flexibility normally comes at the cost of lower performance in calculations.

Machine Code: A sequence of *bytes* that can be executed by the *processor*. Native code compilers produce machine code as output.

`MAXINT`: The largest integer value that can be stored on a computer. It is about half of 2 raised to the power of the number of bits used.

Message: In an object-oriented programming context, the stimulus sent from one object to another to initiate an action on the receiving object. The action is normally the invocation of a method.

Modulo Operator: An operator that finds the remainder of an integer division. Not to be confused with *modulus*.

Modulus: The size of something. For example, the modulus of both 5 and -5 is 5.

Object: *See Instance.*

Object Code: The *machine code* representation of the program *source code.* Often the object code will be stored in a number of files, one per module, and these files will be linked together to form an *executable program.*

Operator Precedence: The set of rules that a programming language uses to determine which operators will be executed first in the event of a conflict. Most languages follow the normal mathematical rules, but some use simple left-to-right order. Also some nonmathematical operators (such as bitwise operators) may not have the precedence you might expect.

Parameter: A placeholder used in defining a function or method. The parameter is considered by the function to be a local variable. When the function is called, the parameter takes on the values of the *arguments* passed in from the calling code.

P-Code: A form of portable object code that is particularly easy and fast to translate into machine code. It allows a single translator to perform the relatively complex translation from source code to P-code. A multitude of simpler, platform-specific, P-code to machine code translators are then possible. This type of translation is the principle behind many modern languages, including Python and Java.

PDL: *P*rogram *D*escription *L*anguage. A formally defined pseudocode. It has rules similar to those of a normal programming language but with greater flexibility in defining new names and a less rigid syntax. I find a much more informal pseudocode to be sufficiently expressive; it rarely causes confusion.

Platform: The combination of computer hardware and operating system in use. Most platforms have commonly understood meanings, even though they may not be technically correct. For example, a PC platform implies an IBM PC clone with the Microsoft Windows operating system. A Linux platform implies an IBM PC clone with Linux installed. Thus the PC could use either Linux or Windows—but the latter is assumed. Similarly, Linux could be installed on a Sparc, Alpha, or MIPS processor—but a PC is assumed. If you are using another variation you need to specify exactly your combination of hardware and operating system. When reporting problems on newgroups or mailing lists, it's a good idea to specify which platform you are using.

Precision: The number of digits in a floating-point number that are reliable.

Process: (1) The sequence of steps required to perform some task. (2) A running program. Some programs will consist of more than one process when they start. Most operating systems provide tools to enable the user to view the currently running processes. On Linux/UNIX, this tool is the ps command. On Windows 95/98, it is the CTRL-ALT-DEL key combination. On Windows NT4, it is the Task Manager accessed via the context menu on the taskbar.

Processor: The component within a computer that executes the *machine code* instructions found in an *executable program*. Many modern computers have multiple processors, allowing several programs or *processes* to run concurrently.

Pseudocode: An informal description of a program. It may resemble the target programming language to a greater or lesser extent. It should indicate clearly the four basic constructs of programming, but has no formal rules of syntax or grammar to worry about.

Raise: Generate an exception that can be *caught* elsewere in the program by an *exception handler*.

Random Access: The ability to access a file via an index. Thus, instead of searching from the start of the file, the program will jump to wherever the indexed data lives in the file. Sometimes restrictions on random access exist—for example, all of the lines in the file may need to be equal lengths. Also, writing to such a file may cause problems if the new data is longer than the original. Where random access is applicable, however, it is a very fast access mechanism when dealing with long files. Note that the index information is often stored in a separate file or files.

Real: *See floating point.*

Registry: A special set of data files used by Windows to store system configuration information. Many programs store user preferences and similar information there. Windows provides low-level system calls to access the Registry but WSH provides an easier-to-use object-level interface.

Run: To execute a program.

Shell Script: A file of instructions executed by a command prompt in UNIX. Such command prompts are called shells, with the official Posix standard being the korn shell. Each shell has its own syntax, although they are mostly similar. Shell scripts have all the features of programming languages and are used for the same type of tasks as *WSH* or *DOS* BAT files.

Signed Integer: *See also integer.* Integers are signed by default in that they can take on positive or negative values. Compare *Unsigned Integer.*

Slicing (Lists): The ability to reference a segment of a list. In Python, this task is accomplished by using an index comprising two values separated by a colon. The first value is the first element of the slice, and the second value is the element after the slice—the same convention as used for the `range()` function's parameters.

Source Code: The text of a program as typed in by the programmer.

Standard Library: The set of functions that are built in to a programming language or that are supplied in modules packaged with the standard distribution. Programmers can safely assume that they can use functions from the standard library without fear that they will not work on another computer or platform with the same language installed.

Structured Programming: The set of rules and principles that allow us to organize programs. Some of these guidelines include the desirability of having a single entry and exit point for each function, and avoiding the use of global variables where possible. This book has tried to pass on some of the principles behind structured programming. Recent studies have shown that some of the ideas enshrined in structured programming may not be quite as universally true as was once thought, however.

Syntax: The rules covering the layout and "punctuation" of a programming language. The syntax describes which keywords should be used, and when. It includes issues like when and where to use brackets or semicolons. One way that you know you are becoming fluent in a programming language is when the majority of your errors are no longer syntax errors!

Syntax Coloring: Some text editors can color the text to match the syntax of the language—for example, strings in one color, keywords in another, and comments in yet another. This simple device turns out to be a very powerful tool for spotting syntax errors!

Tcl: *Tool Control Language.* It spawned a GUI toolkit called Tk, which is used by the Tkinter module that ships with Python.

Throw: *See Raise.*

Translator: *See Compiler, Interpreter.*

Unix: An extremely influential operating system that has a close affinity with the way programmers work. The UNIX environment is probably the best software development environment ever created. UNIX is extremely terse and unfriendly on first acquaintance, but once mastered it becomes addictive. This multitasking, multiuser operating system is very stable. *Linux* is a free, UNIX-like, and increasingly popular operating system.

Unsigned Integer: An integer that can take on only positive values.

Variable: A named reference to data.

Video Driver: The software that controls the video hardware in a PC. It implements the operating system *API* for the specific hardware installed.

Whitespace: Invisible printable characters, such as tabs, spaces, and line-feeds. Some programming languages ignore whitespace; others, including Python, treat some whitespace as important—specifically, the indentation level.

WSH: *Windows Script Host*. An object model and programming environment for Windows that enables programmers to easily access the system *registry* and files. It is considerably more powerful than the older MS-DOS batch files. WSH as provided by Microsoft can interpret VBScript and JScript but the capability is there for other languages to be used as well. Both Python and Perl have options that allow them to be used with WSH.

Index

Register Your Book

at www.aw.com/cseng/register

You may be eligible to receive:

- Advance notice of forthcoming editions of the book
- Related book recommendations
- Chapter excerpts and supplements of forthcoming titles
- Information about special contests and promotions throughout the year
- Notices and reminders about author appearances, tradeshows, and online chats with special guests

Contact us

If you are interested in writing a book or reviewing manuscripts prior to publication, please write to us at:

Editorial Department
Addison-Wesley Professional
75 Arlington Street, Suite 300
Boston, MA 02116 USA
Email: AWPro@aw.com

Visit us on the Web: http://www.aw.com/cseng

CD-ROM WARRANTY

What's on the CD?

For a detailed outline, see the file README.TXT in the CD root directory. This appendix attempts to provide an outline view of what to expect.

Python

The Python directory tree has all of the Python-related files. These files include the source code for most of the longer examples in the book as well as various installable packages from the Python Web site.

code

The source code area is subdivided to match the sections of the book. Thus Section4 contains the source code from the case studies. The code will not always exactly match that in the book. For example, it may contain some extra comments. There is also the code for the game of mastermind as suggested, but not described, in Chapter 23.

downloads

The downloads directory contains the download files for Python, the Windows extensions, the latest version of IDLE, a GUI builder for Tkinter, and my on-line tutorial, which started the project in the first place.

Tools

The tools folder contains the RCS configuration management system. RCS does not have an especially user-friendly installation package, so you should read the README files carefully.

Other Languages

The Other Languages subtree contains the source code used in Appendix B to illustrate other languages. It also contains tutorials for many of these languages and, in a few cases, an installable version of the language. Each language has its own folder, which contains separate folders for the source code and tutorials as appropriate.

All material previously distributed by CD-ROM is now
available at http://www.awprofessional.com